Motorcycle Touring

in

Prince Edward Island

...your guide to tip to tip adventure

by:
Julie V. Watson
with
John C. Watson

Seacroft
www.seacroftpei.com

Copyright © Julie V. Watson 2008
Revised Edition - 2010/ Second printing

Seacroft
P.O. Box 1204,
Charlottetown, PE, Canada C1A 7M8
Email: biz@seacroftpei.com
Web: www.seacroftpei.com

Editorial Content: Julie V. Watson
Design: Julie V. Watson
Production facilitator: Pollywog Desktop Designs
Photography: John C. Watson, or
                Julie V. Watson unless otherwise noted
Cover design and photography: John C. Watson, Imagemaker Studio www.imps.ca
Editorial Contributors: Debbie Gamble
                John C. Watson

Library and Archives Canada Cataloguing in Publication

Watson, Julie V. 1943-
Motorcycle Touring in Prince Edward Island...your guide to tip to tip adventure / Julie V. Watson
ISBN 978-0-9687092-8-3

Motorcycling, Prince Edward Island, Canada, travel / tour guide

www.seacroftpei.com

What's Inside

Welcome to our Prince Edward Island guide book designed especially for those who enjoy motorcycle touring. We hope you find our book useful and enjoy your visit to one of the world's great Islands.

Photo courtesy Murray Fraser

Keeping up to date

*Want to know what rides, rallies, and special events
are in the near future?*

*Like to hook up with local riders through
club meets, rides and such?*

*Looking for a warm welcome at accommodations,
eateries, nightlife?*

*Like to keep up with news and views of
the motorcycle community?*

Check out
www.motorcyclepei.com
and our blog
blog.motorcyclepei.com

*Take it National .....
for a look at great rides and experiences
across this great nation visit*
www.motorcycle-touring-Canada.net

Introduction

A short sail on a ferry, or an even shorter ride across one of the world's unique bridges, brings you and your bike to the shores of Prince Edward Island. Nestled in the southern Gulf of St. Lawrence in Atlantic Canada the country's smallest province is a place to relax, to enjoy uncrowded roads, magnificent scenery and a warm welcome.

Your first glimpse of the island will be an emerald green landscape, rimmed by red sandstone cliffs and beaches, and surrounded by the blue waters of Northumberland Straight. It beckons you to explore.

With 'roads less travelled' winding through beautiful countryside Prince Edward Island has become home to a thriving motorcycle community and a popular destination for touring enthusiasts from across North America - and beyond. Enthusiasts enjoy the fresh open air, being part of the environment around them. It's the scents, the feel of mist on the face, the oneness with nature; a feeling described by some as soaring the highways and byways with the two-wheel machine beneath them becoming an extension of their body as they sweep around curves and settle into straight-aways.

Touring is so easily enjoyed. With the countryside never more than 15 minutes away from any downtown and little traffic congestion the Island is attracting more and more touring motorcyclists each summer. Some haul their bikes behind an RV, others pack what they need in saddlebags and enjoy the adventure of the road.

Visitor or local, they are as diverse as the bikes they ride. Many enjoy a solitary experience. Others ride two-up with a soul mate behind. Still others enjoy organized group runs taking pleasure from traveling with like-minded people and mastering the skills required to ride in formation.

The sense of camaraderie is hard to equal. The common bond is strong, although enthusiasts do break down into their own unique interests. For some it is roads travelled and adventures lived. For others it is the mechanics of the bike. Yet others are bonded through type of bike, be it Gold Wing, Harley-Davidson, or one of the others. Conversation inevitably turns to how they run, and the fine tuning that makes each one unique to its owner. Some want clean pavement, others are into backroading challenges. Whatever your passion you can enjoy it in Prince Edward Island

Just 64 km (40 miles) across at its widest point, and 280 km (175 miles) from the eastern to western tip as the crow flies, this is a great place to come, explore and enjoy your vacation. Nothing is far away, yet the trip to get there is filled with good riding through scenery that is beautiful and ever changing.

Many first time visitors are surprised at the rolling hills that predominate, especially in the central region. Our altitude ranges from sea-level to 494 ft, with Springton taking honours as the highest spot in the province. Travellers here rarely see flat roads ahead, and when they do, they don't last long. Makes for a powerful riding experience.

Scenic vistas range from the patchwork-like fields of an active agricultural community in rural areas, through scenic coastal drives with charming fishing villages, and neat tidy, towns and cities that marry historic treasures with modern amenities. Sound a bit like an advertising message? I guess so, but its true. Although Prince Edward Island has the modern amenities and services that matter, we are less populated, less industrialized, less hurried; leaving more for the preservation and enjoyment of traditional values and links with both the rural community and the cultural component of life as Islanders.

About Prince Edward Island

Prince Edward Island is a unique place of great beauty. Some say it sits like jewel in the sea. Ocean waves lap against a shoreline comprised of a mix of red or white sand beaches, red, wind sculpted cliffs and magnificent headlands. Coastal villages, home ports to inshore fishermen and women, lighthouses and working harbours, speak to the close relationship between Islanders and the sea.

Rolling green hills and woodlands dominate a rural landscape that is home to a flourishing agricultural industry. Dairy and beef cattle, row upon row of potatoes, and numerous mixed farms, often with an organic focus, are the heart of the Island farming community.

Villages, towns and our two cities reflect community pride in place and offer a pleasing mix of preserved historic buildings and modern amenities. With an economy driven by agriculture, tourism, fishing and then manufacturing, Islanders place high importance on the environment and caring for both land and the sea.

Come to the Island for a vacation. You'll soon find yourself relaxed, refreshed and ready to take on life's challenges. Here you can enjoy a day at the beach, explore miles of coastline, walk on nature trails, meander along scenic roads, tour to lighthouses, check in then enjoy a night out on the town, eat meals to talk about or be entertained by talented performers. We may be small, but there is a lot of 'doing' packed into Canada's smallest province.

Originally named Epekwitk, an Aboriginal name meaning land cradled on the waves, by the Island's first residents, the Mi'kmaq, Prince Edward Island is a unique place of great beauty. Pronunciation of the Mi'kmaq name was changed to Abegweit by European settlers.

Jacques Cartier discovered the Island in 1534. The French called it Ile Saint-Jean. When the British gained control they changed the name to St. John's Island. In 1799 the Island renamed itself for the father of Queen Victoria, Prince Edward, Duke of Kent. We kept that one.

With miles of coastline the Island offers many opportunities to enjoy solitude during a walk on the shore. Here, at Seal Cove near Murray Harbour, seals are often spotted swimming or basking in the sun on a sandbar. Mussel farmers share the waterway with recreational boaters and awesome birdlife. Eagles, heron, seabirds and songbirds all did fly-bys over our campsite.

Prince Edward Island is especially enjoyable for those who enjoy traveling and exploring roads with less traffic and a slower pace. The Island has no multi-lane highways. Generally roads are paved and in good condition although we won't deny the presence of potholes and broken pavement, especially in the spring.

You really can't get lost on the Island, all roads eventually lead to Summerside or Charlottetown - but picking up a map (and if you are like me and tend to try to read while a passenger - a spare!) at a Visitor Information Centre as you arrived via bridge or ferry is a grand idea.

Scenic drives take you to secluded coves, quaint fishing villages; past stunning dunes, beaches and wind sculpted cliffs.

Heritage Roads are for those who enjoy a little backroading. Traditional red-clay, they are protected by the Scenic Heritage Road program and retain names passed down by generations of local residents: Jack's Road is a favourite because my husband like's having his name on a beautiful country lane. A mandatory buffer zone preserves the link these roads have with the past. Many pass through canopy's formed by trees and are beautiful, especially in the fall.

These roads can be rutted and slippery after wet weather so beware. All are marked on the highway map by a symbol with two trees on a brown background. Another great photo op!

Our roads are not bordered by billboards and signage, a move by the government to protect the unspoiled scenic beauty. It makes for scenic vistas, but does make it a bit hard to find particular tourism operators. Watch for standardized information signs, in blue or green near intersections.

We caught up with these riders enjoying a break after a run on this clay road found near St. Ann. A picture perfect fall day.

Caution: If you are the type to enjoy backroading please pay careful attention to signage and avoid logging roads or private roads. They can deteriorate quickly, especially if it rains. Never try riding a clay or dirt road in the rain on a bike not designed for off roading.

> You may think of Prince Edward Island as small, but we have 5,648 km (3,530 mi) of roads to travel.

You can be as active as you wish. Laze on the beach - we have miles to choose from. Or perhaps you prefer to be more physical, kayaking, deep sea fishing, frolicking in the surf, windsurfing, or boating. Or the land based activities: golf, exploring, hiking one of many walking trails, fly or rod fishing, bowling, shopping, mini-golf, horseback riding or more. Heck building sand castles might be as 'active' as you want to get.

Or, you can kick back. Spread your blanket on a beach and just laze with the surf as your music. Pitch your tent on a shadded campsite and while away the hours chatting with friends. Pull up a chair in one of our night spots or go to one of our great on-stage performances, linger over a fine meal, or eat lobster on a wharf.

Enjoy being pampered at a resort, choose a fine motel, or get back to nature by camping. No matter how you like to spend your vacation, it's fine, with us. No pressures here!

General Information

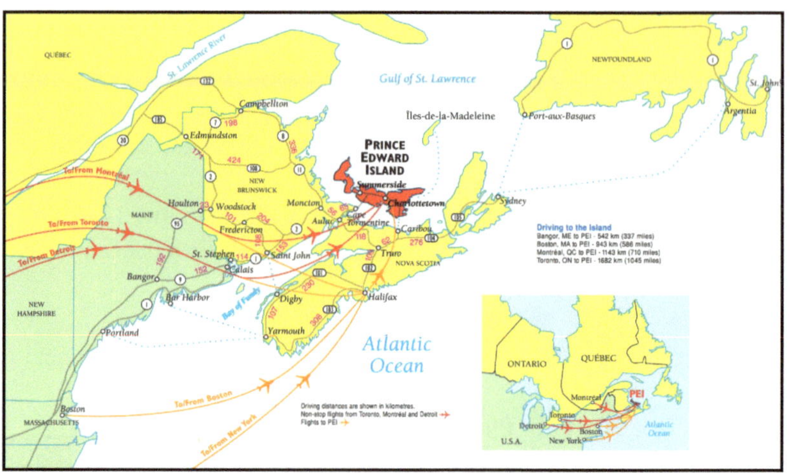

LOCATION:

Nestled in the Gulf of St. Lawrence on Canada's eastern seaboard, Prince Edward Island is one of four provinces comprising Atlantic Canada, one of three known as the Maritimes. It is easily accessed via New Brunswick or Nova Scotia by crossing Northumberland Strait.

ALTITUDE:

Sea-level to 152 m (494 ft), the highest point is at Springton, in Queens County

SIZE:

280 km (175 mi) long (tip to tip as the crow flies) and 6 to 64 km (4 to 40 mi) wide. Because of this variation in width, no one place in the province is more than 16 km (10 mi) from the sea. Sometimes referred to as a million acre farm, the Island is actually 5,656 sq km (2,184 sq mi) or 3,622,400 acres.

POPULATION:

with a population of about 141,000, Prince Edward Island has less people than many Canadian cities. Just over half are considered rural. Of course the "population" swells in the summer as those in the know vacation here.

LANGUAGE:

English is the primary language. French is used in Acadian communities, and provincial and federal services are available in both languages throughout the province.

KEEPING IN TOUCH:

Many accommodations and libraries offer internet connections. In Prince Edward Island you can also connect at Community Access (CAP) sites located in most communities. To find a site near you phone 1-877-686-7458 or before you leave home go to www.peicaps.org and print out the list. Access is free, or inexpensive, and other services such as fax are available.

. Time Zone is: Atlantic ET +1; GMT -4 (depending on season)
. The area code for the province is 902

HEALTHCARE:

Large hospitals with full Emergency care are located in Charlottetown and Summerside. Smaller hospitals are located in Montague, Souris, Alberton, O'Leary, Tyne Valley. Health clinics offering walk-in service are also located in Charlottetown, Summerside, O'Leary, Kensington and Montague. Check the telephone directory yellow pages for locations and hours of operation.

Everyone, particularly Non-Canadian residents, should ensure that they have adequate health care insurance before leaving home. Make sure you carry your health coverage documentation with you.

After getting caught in an early December snow storm our Distribution guy, Jack, was glad to be welcomed home by the family canine.

RIDING SEASON:

Although the occasional die-hard claims to ride in every month of the year, reality is that riding season in Prince Edward Island is usually May thru October. Spring is vibrant with colour, particularly in June when temperatures range from 8 to 22 degrees Celcious (45-70 F). Summer can be hot, but not so hot or humid as to be unpleasant. It is rare for the temperature to soar above 32 C (90 F). For many Autumn is the most magnificent season. The air is crisp, the atmosphere bright, the landscape seems to glory in temperatures similar to spring.

SHOPPING:

Small shops are easily found in villages and towns throughout Prince Edward Island. Larger stores, malls and downtown districts are found in Charlottetown and Summerside. Most major stores and malls are open 7-days a week during riding season.

Two taxes are collected on most purchases and services: a provincial sales tax of 10%, which is calculated on the total of the price plus the goods and services tax and GST. This is a good place to shop for clothing, footwear and books as no provincial tax is charged

SERVICES:

Banks and ATMs are plentiful, as are gas stations and other services. Prince Edward Island has pretty much everything you will need, just on a smaller scale than more highly populated areas. Everything else can be ordered in from away if need be, with couriers providing excellent service.

RECYCLING:

Islanders recycle and can get quite annoyed with folks who don't follow the rules of garbage disposal. So dedicated are they to recycling, Statistics Canada says Prince Edward Island leads the country for household access and use of recycling and composting programs. As you ride our highways and byways you will be impressed by the cleanliness. This is a result of an Island-wide cleanup which sees residents out cleaning the ditches and roadsides in May, after the snows have gone.

We ask that you do your part to keep our Island pristine. Garbage cans will be labeled compost, recyclables and waste, often with descriptions in the form of symbols or pictures. Use them, and do follow the rule of never leaving anything behind. Carry your garbage out until you find the correct container to put it in.

Littering is not condoned

SMOKING & ALCOHOL:

Smoking is prohibited in public places. Alcohol can only be purchased in Liquor Commission outlets, found in most communities, and licensed bars and restaurants. Drinking and riding is not permitted.

Getting Here

Prince Edward Island is located on the east coast of Canada, on the southern side of the Gulf of St. Lawrence. The island is cradled by Nova Scotia to the south east and New Brunswick to the south west, separated from the mainland by Northumberland Strait. Just a few hours drive from Maine in the U.S.A., or any point in Nova Scotia or New Brunswick Prince Edward Island is a wonderful destination from anywhere in North America.

CROSSING THE STRAIT

Whether you arrive by ferry or drive across our bridge you are going to have to pay. Fortunately the fares and/or tolls are not too steep, and they don't charge you to arrive. Tolls are only collected when you leave

John Watson photo

PHOTO TIP - For a terrific shot of the bridge when arriving from New Brunswick, proceed through Gateway Village to the stop sign beside the Esso Station. Turn right and drive through the village of Borden to a small park under the base of the bridge. A lighthouse marks the best spot for photos. The continuation of the road once led to the loading ramps to the ferry before the bridge opened. The area now houses a mussel processing plant. Or turn left onto Rte 10 as you leave town. Along this road you can get a terrific view of the whole bridge as it curves across the Strait. Here you can get a great photo of the bridge, and a better sense of how great a project building it was.

FROM NEW BRUNSWICK

Confederation Bridge provides an easy road link between Cape Jourimain, New Brunswick and Borden-Carleton, Prince Edward Island. The 12.9 km (9 mile) crossing takes you up and over Northumberland Strait where you get a magnificent first-look at the Island. On days when the sky is blue, beautiful white clouds hang in the sky and waves wash upon the shore, you understand how it earned its native name Abegweit (meaning cradled on the waves), from our first citizens, the Mi'kmaq .

Its fascinating to see sea gulls riding the air currents beside the bridge, keeping up with traffic with barely a flap of their wings. You will see fishing boats and occasionally a larger vessel.

As you come down off the bridge bear right to Gateway Village. Here you will find a Visitor Information Centre which will provide a map, Visitor Guide, and much more information.

In the same building there is a display of how the bridge was built. Shops, eateries and a liquor store are all nearby. Do drop in to Cavendish Figurines right across the road - a fun place where you can get some fun photos, see figurines being made and find great souvenirs.

Confederation Bridg from New Brunswick

Confederation Bridge is the longest continuous span bridge in the world over water that is covered with ice for several months of the year. Of course that won't affect bikers who have more sense than to travel on two wheels in the dead of winter. The bridge is open year round, 24 hours a day unless winds are very high or weather creates unsafe traveling conditions.

A relaxing way of getting to the Island from Caribou (near Pictou), Nova Scotia, a 75-minute ferry voyage lets you enjoy the experience of being on the water. Watch for fishing boats and marine mammals such as seals, whales or dolphin (the latter are very rare sightings, but its exciting if you happen to be lucky). The scenery is wonderful. The ferries have onboard cafeterias and lounges. Once you arrive in Wood Islands you will find a Visitor Information Centre just a short ride beyond the compound. Pick up maps, a Visitors Guide, and check for events and festivities happening during your stay. There is also a gift shop and liquor store.

Ferries cross up to nine times a day for 8 months of the year (early May to mid December), weather permitting. Traveling by motorcycle usually means you don't have to worry about getting on board, but if you are in a hurry you might want to check out a reservation by calling toll-free 1-877-635-7245, or going to www.nfl-bay.com

In 2010 fares for a motorcycle were $45. (Passengers included) and $69 for a motorcycle and trailer or sidecar. *see below

Wood Islands Ferry Terminal takes you into the eastern part of the province. From here you can take a one hour run into Charlottetown, along Rte. l, or take our eastern tour.

TIPS - Don't rush to line up for a meal. The crossing takes more than an hour so head for the outer deck first to watch as the boat travels past the shoreline for open water. You'll pass by the fishing wharf, see lots of sea birds on the channel markers and shore, and enjoy some good photo ops. Once past the Caribou Island Lighthouse you'll find lineups at the cafeteria gone and have lots of time for refreshments.

* - Since they only charge to leave Prince Edward Island you may want to arrive by ferry from Nova Scotia, and leave by Confederation Bridge to New Brunswick. It will save you dollars ($17 vs $45 or $69). Of course gas costs may negate that if you are heading for Halifax, rather than into New Brunswick.

John Watson photo

PHOTO TIP - *after leaving the ferry compound, take a hard right. This road, which takes you back towards the dock area, meanders around to Wood Island's Provincial Park. This is a great place to get some good photos of the ferry, your bike and fishing boats. There is also a charming lighthouse museum and gift shop. Well worth a look before you head on down the road*

FROM THERE TO HERE

The Island is an easy destination that will take you through beautiful riding country as you make your way here through our sister provinces of Nova Scotia or New Brunswick. Check these riding distances:

From Toronto, Ontario - 1682 km (1045 miles)
From Montreal, Quebec - 1143 km (710 miles)
From Bangor, Maine - 542 km (337 miles)
From Boston, Mass - 943 km (586 miles)

PRINCE EDWARD ISLAND TOURIST
 INFORMATION
Tourism PEI, Box 940, Charlottetown, PEI,
Canada   C1A 7M5
902 368-5540   Toll free: 1-800-463-4PEI
gentleisland@gov.pe.ca
www.gentleisland.com

CONFEDERATION BRIDGE
www.confederationbridge.com

NORTHUMBERLAND FERRY
www.peiferry.com
for fares, schedules, reservations:
www.nfl-bay.com
1-877-635-7245

VISITOR INFORMATION CENTRES
No matter whether you arrive by bridge or ferry you
will find a warm welcome and loads of travel information at a Visitor Information Centre located just a
short drive from your arrival point. Do drive in and
pick up a free map and Island Guide.

There are VICs located in:
> Summerside
> Mount Pleasant
> Cavendish
> Charlottetown
> St. Peters
> Souris
> Borden Carleton
> Wood Islands

EXTENDING THE ADVENTURE

As an island Prince Edward Island doesn't look like it is the route to anywhere except back to the mainland. How-
ever, each year many bikers incorporate a side trip to Iles de la Madeleine, in Quebec, into their Island trip.
From Souris you are just a ferry crossing away. For information:
1-877-624-4437 (tourism)   www.tourismeilesdelamadeleine.com
1-888-986-3278 (ferry)   www.ctma.ca

Interesting to know.....what we are made of

One of the most distinguishing things about PEI is the rich red earth. As you ride
in from the bridge or ferry one of the first things you notice about the landscape
is the rich red soil, ploughed into ribs which catch the sun and shadows as the
day progresses. From spring, through summer and into fall these fields are
capped with lush green potato plants. It's a beautiful sight to see. And this soil,
perfect for growing potatoes among other things, is said to be our most important natural resource.The redness, which contrasts so well with the blue of the
sea and sky, and greens and golds of fields and forests, is due to a high iron-
oxide content - yup its rust! Fact is the Island is sedimentary bed rock, a soft,
red sandstone. Pretty fragile as rock goes, it crumbles and breaks down into our
red soil.

For a look at
this bed rock,
and how the elements affect it just head to the shore
and check out the sandstone cliffs. Rain, snow and
wind sculpt them into beautiful sights to behold. If
you love it, take a photo, for surely next time you
come back the elements will have brought about
change!

Lets Go Touring!!

LIGHTHOUSE TOUR

Lighthouses are an integral part of Prince Edward Island history, and of marine activity to this day. Some of the almost 50 that dot our shoreline are accessible to the public, providing viewpoints which are always worth a visit. Many are marked on the provinces highway map.

Lighthouses are a great destination for anyone interested in a tour which explores coastal Prince Edward Island. First a little background.

The sea brought the first European settlers to our shores beginning in the 1700s. They soon realized the importance of navigational aids and built lighthouses, and range lights to safely guide ships. Each has individual markings visible in day time, and flash light patterns for night. Most modern sailors don't need lighthouses thanks to technology like GPS and radar, however they are part of the heritage and an in-place backup system for modern technology. They are also beautiful.

Lighthouses are preserved and maintained by the Prince Edward Island Lighthouse Society, the Canadian Coast Guard and other agencies, and non-profit groups. The Society works to ensure the safekeeping of the buildings, artifacts and records.

Generally speaking lights shaped like an octagon were built before 1873. After that wood became more scarce and lights were of square construction.

Seven lighthouses open to the public during the summer, are a great basis for a tour. Or, take the challenge of a tip-to-tip tour, riding from North Cape in the west to East Point in the east without following the coastline (275 km / 171 miles one way). You can do this in a day, but keep in mind you have to add on getting to your planned start point and return - with much to see along the way.

This is where you need your map. Plan your own route to suite time available and your start point.

The following lighthouses open for visitors during the summer. We have listed them from west to east, along the province's south shore:

West Point
Victoria
Point Prim
Wood Islands
Cape Bear
Panmure Head
East Point

After arriving at East Point, the true lighthouse afficionado will turn their sights west and head back to North Cape for a true around the Island experience. Best spread over a few days so that you can take time to savour the scenery, relax and explore sites, the trip takes you past many more lighthouses. The museums are great, bringing to life the stories of lightkeepers, mariners, and indeed history itself.

CAUTION: - When leaving the highway to reach lighthouse sites watch the lanes in from the pavement, puddles may hide fairly deep dips as most roads are sand or clay. They can be slow riding challenges, but not impassable so just take it easy. Parking usually will not be paved so choose your spot.

WEST POINT LIGHTHOUSE

One of the best Island destinations for a real taste of life beside the sea. This unique lighthouse (it's the only stripped light in the province) gives a real look at the past in its museum. Climb to the top - yes right up to the light itself, for a stupendous view. You can see New Brunswick on a clear day. To really appreciate it, take time to read up on the folklore, about shipwrecks and the history. Then take a walk in the woods or along the beach. The lighthouse staff also operate a great restaurant where you can enjoy lobster or home cooking beside the nearby marina. Fishing boats come and go. Visit the craft shop. Lazy on the beach, or go beachcombing.

DIRECTIONS - Take Route 2 west from Summerside. At Carleton follow road signs to West Point. This will take you to Route 14. From Route 14 follow signs to Cedar Dunes Provincial Park. You'll see the black and white striped lighthouse looming above the trees.

BONUS - Plan an overnight here. The lighthouse has been converted into a charming country inn with rooms overlooking the beach. Check the accommodations section and book ahead!   Its popular. Campers will be delighted to find Cedar Dunes Provincial Park right next to the lighthouse. Great beach and walking trails. A restaurant and gift shop at the   wharf just a short walk away.

A fragile dune system is all that protects West Point Lighthouse and Inn from the wrath of the sea and stormy weather. Please stay on designation walkways or trails to the beach.

VICTORIA RANGELIGHT

We mention this lighthouse because it houses a museum, and is located in the charming village of Victoria, aka Victoria-By-The-Sea. It is unique for having two different lights in one structure, and is one of four lights guiding mariners into Victoria Harbour

Do take time to stroll the wharf and the village. There is a great chocolate shop, wonderful theatre and some super, if small, eateries.

DIRECTION - from Route 1 (the TransCanada Highway) heading east from Borden-Carleton, follow the signs to Victoria, just as you leave Crapaud. The lighthouse is small, so head for the wharf and look east. It lies just before the bridge, and Victoria Provincial Park.

POINT PRIM

The oldest lighthouse in the province is also one of the few constructed of brick in Canada. Now covered with wood shingles, you have to go inside to see the brick. Round, it has been in service since 1846. This is a great spot for some R&R. Climb to the top, take a tour, enjoy historic maritime displays. Peaceful

DIRECTIONS - Follow Route 1 (the TransCanada Highway) east from Charlottetown towards Wood Island Ferry. Between Eldon and Pinette turn south (right) onto Route 209 and follow it to the end. Go left, through the woods to the lighthouse.

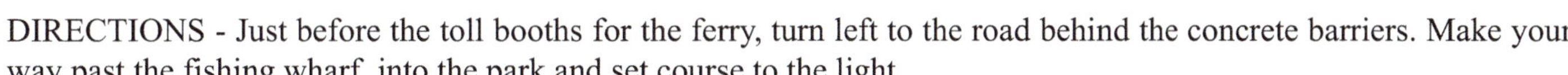

WOOD ISLAND LIGHTHOUSE

People tend to over look this lighthouse, found to the east of the ferry terminal.

photo supplied by Wood Island Lighthouse

Everyone is so focused on catching the boat they pass by the great stop that is right in plain sight. The light was built in 1876 as an aid to both Marine and fishing vessels. When the ferry service to Pictou, Nova Scotia started it took on an even greater navigational role.

Inside you will find the Lighthouse Interpretive Museum and Fisheries Museum along with nine other themed rooms, including a Nautical Craft Shop. Ask them about the recent "move." The whole lighthouse was picked up and moved because of coastal erosion. Outside you will find a great spot to put the kick stand down and just laze in the sunshine. Watch the ferry come and go, enjoy sea breezes and sun shine. This is one of those 'its great to be alive' places.

DIRECTIONS - Just before the toll booths for the ferry, turn left to the road behind the concrete barriers. Make your way past the fishing wharf, into the park and set course to the light.

CAPE BEAR LIGHTHOUSE

It is said that the first to hear and record distress signals from the Titanic was the keeper at Cape Bear. A museum occupies the site that was one of just a few Marconi Wireless Stations built to facilitate communication between government vessels in the early 1900s. This one was charged with keeping ice breakers between Pictou, Nova Scotia, Georgetown, and Charlottetown on course. During WWII they looked for, and found German U-boats. Today the view is amazing. Take a picnic and stay a while.

DIRECTIONS - Travel east from Wood Islands, along route 18 through White Sands and Guernsey Cove. When the pavement takes a sharp left, continue along the dirt road to the second lane on the right. Watch for the sign to the lighthouse.

PANMURE HEAD LIGHTHOUSE

This lighthouse stands at the entrance to Georgetown Harbour and Cardigan Bay. Located on Panmure Island it is a great destination. The road to the Lighthouse passes by Panmure Island Provincial Park with a spectacular beach. On a clear day you can see the hills of Nova Scotia in the distance. CAUTION: When you get on Panmure Island, particularly in the area with marsh on one side of the road and sand dunes on the other, slow down, keep your eye peeled for clam and other shells on the road. Seagulls carry shellfish high in the sky then drop them onto the pavement. They can puncture tires.

photo supplied by Tourism PEI

DIRECTIONS - East of Montague, follow Route 17, turning off onto Route 347. After crossing the causeway at Panmure Provincial Park, follow the second driveway to the right towards the lighthouse.

EAST POINT LIGHTHOUSE

Prince Edward Island's most easterly point is guarded by the East Point Light. Built in 1867 it has been on the move ever since. As one of our most itinerant lighthouses the octagon shaped wooden tower has been moved more than once. First it was relocated after a ship-wreck determined it was positioned wrong. Later erosion caused more moves. The light was automated in 1989. This is an awesome place to be at first light when the sun rises over the ocean. At low tide get a glimpse of the rocky off-shore sea bottom which has been the cause of many shipwrecks. Park your bike and walk along the tops of the cliffs (stay back from the edges) for spectacular views which may well include the ferry plying the waters between Souris and Iles de la Madeleine.

DIRECTIONS - Follow your map to the eastern tip of the Island. From Route 16 turn east onto a paved road marked East Point Light.

Photographers Tip: East Point Lighthouse from the south, gives a far different image than from the north. John Watson photos

Tip to tip Touring

One of the really cool things that pavement huggers like to do is a tip to tip run from East Point - obviously the eastern tip, to North Cape, not quite as obviously the western tip. Lighthouse to lighthouse the distance is 275 km, or 171 miles, so it is certainly a "doable" day run taking about 3 hours and 45 minutes in the saddle. Of course you have to be at one of the ends of the Island to start your run, and when you get to the other end, you have to come back, so it isn't quite as easy as it sounds. If you plan the run, check in at the lighthouse before you leave and tell them you are tip-to-tipping. You must obey traffic rules. Drive careful and have fun! Don't forget pictures!

Western P.E.I.

Seeking the Wind – North Cape and Back Again

Western Prince Edward Island offers some of the best riding and scenery you'll find anywhere and a good run can be designed to fit time available. If you only have a day to spare you might want to motor to North Cape and meander back. It's a straight run up Rte 2 from just west of Summerside to Tignish, just a few minutes from the western tip of the Island. Or you can crank up the throttle and do the entire coastal tour in a day if riding, rather than stopping, is your choice. We're assuming that you have been wise enough to allow a couple of days for real vacation time but no worries if you haven't - this run can easily fit into a summer day.

We're assuming that you have been wise enough to allow a couple of days for real vacation time. We'll start our tour in Summerside - the gateway to the North Cape Coastal Drive. Just watch for the North Cape Coastal Drive road markers. The government has done a great job of marking the route.

A stop at the Acadian Museum in Miscouche (on Rte. 2, on the north side of Summerside) will prepare you for a visit to the Acadian region of Evangeline. Not necessary, but an introduction to the Acadian culture. As you head out on your coastal adventure, remember you are traveling rural roads which may be a little rough in places. Keep those eyes peeled and take care. To take a fast run to Tignish stay on Rte 2. Otherwise follow our directions below.

Travel west on Rte. 11 to follow the south shore into the Evangeline region where the Acadian culture thrives. If you luck into one of their festivals you are in for great music, good times and great eats. Continue on Rte 11 until you reach a junction with Rte 2 and turn left towards Tignish. Just a few minutes down the road turn right on Rte 136. If you need a break turn into Mill River Provincial Park. A resort offers refreshments, boating or even a game of golf. Back out to Rte. 136, turn left until you meet up with Rte 12, then turn left again. Your destination is Northport.

Northport   *John Watson photo*

When you reach the town of Alberton, once home to a thriving silver fox industry with a museum to tell you all about it, watch carefully for signs to Northport, one of the Island's prettiest fishing villages. You can eat at the pier, shop and just plain enjoy the peace, quiet and spirit of place. Check out the interpretive centre to learn about a daring sea rescue and shipwreck.

Head back to Rte 12 and travel north to North Cape. This magical western tip of the Island has much to see and do (for a hint see the photos). Those heavy horses in the fields are used to drag rakes through the surf to harvest Irish Moss. It's a sight to see!

North Cape itself is a must stop. Do plan to stay a while. This is home to the longest natural rock reef in North America. At low tide you can walk out on the top of the reef for a magical close to nature experience. Seals often swim along side, you can hear fishermen talking nearby on a calm day, and sea birds glide above.

For the environmentally minded there is a Wind Energy Interpretive

Centre with an exhibit on net metering and the wind hydrogen applications on site. Its all rounded out with spectacular "end of the island" views of the cliffs, nature trails, a lighthouse, the Wind and Reef Restaurant (good food and spectacular view) and a gift shop.

North Cape Interpretive Centre (top photo) is home to an interpretive centre, restaurant overlooking the reef, gift shop, wind farm, walking trails It's an Island gem - a fascinating place to visit.

Travel back to Tignish, a great place to overnight, or continue on to North Cape, which is spectacular at sunrise and sunset! as well as beaches and such. We recommend Tignish Heritage Inn, behind the St. Simon and St. Jude Church. Built in 1868, it has been lovingly restored and features beautiful gardens. Modern, but with a flavour of the past. Close to Mile '0' of Confederation Trail - a walkers dream.

Pick up Rte 14 in Tignish to travel back via the south shore. You'll pass by Nail Pond (see below). Highlights along the way include Skinner's Pond (Stompin' Tom country) where beaches are awesome, Miminegash, home of Seaweed Pie Café and Irish Moss Interpretation Centre and West Point Lighthouse - (watch the sand in the parking area).

Climb to the top of the Lighthouse and check out the view. On a clear day you can see New Brunswick. This was Canada's first Inn to open in an active lighthouse. Take time to explore the museum's extensive lighthouse exhibits, enjoy a swim from their great beach, or stay overnight. Enjoy a wonderful meal of local seafood, steak or your favourite menu selections in their restaurant which has been relocated to the village wharf area along with a gift shop. Their Chowder is famous! Enjoy a moonlight walk on the beach then fall asleep lulled by the sound of waves at your doorstep.

Tignish Heritage Inn

Irish Moss Harvesting mural

West Point Lighthouse

NAIL POND

This tiny community was the focus of national attention in 2008 when a team from the University of British Columbia came to town to dig up a whale. It was a big deal. A 26-metre female blue whale had been buried here since 1987. The team came to retrieve the skeleton, clean the bones, pack it in a cargo container and ship it 6,000 km to a new home where it will be suspended from the ceiling of a specially built glass atrium at the Beaty Biodiversity Museum.

Why is this noteworthy. Just think of it. No other creature, past or present grows as big as the blue whale. There are only 20 skeletons on display worldwide and this will be the first for Canada. After the whale beached the PEI Government and the Canadian Museum of Nature collaborated to preserve it. For something this big, an estimated 80,000 kilograms, the only viable option was to drag it off the beach, bury it and let nature do its job. Eventually PEI gave the British Columbia University permission to retrieve the skeleton.

I had the experience of seeing whales beached on the shore of Prince Edward Island, and once viewed one from the ferry at Wood Island. Others said it was a dolphin or porpoise however, I choose to remember it as a whale. To me it is miraculous to think that the great creatures swim just off shore of the Island where I live. And one day I will visit the PEI blue in BC.

Take Rte 14 out of West Point and follow road signs to O'Leary. Just about everyone knows that some folks refer to Prince Edward Island as "Spud Island" in recognition of the potatoes that are grown here. You might not think a little museum devoted to potatoes in a small town off the beaten track is worth a visit however the Potato Museum here might just surprise you. The national Amazing Potato Exhibit, Machine Gallery and the O'Leary Community Museum and a gift shop with many things potato can prove fun. They have some neat stuff here, including an iron lung and an old switchboard office. To find it just look for the giant potato in O'Leary. Its not a big place. Follow the North Cape Coastal Drive markers back to Rte 2 and turn right. Now is the time to decide if more exploration is the order of the day, or whether you want a quicker, straighter run back to Summerside.

If exploring is on the agenda turn left on Rte 12 at Portage, travel to Rte 163 and turn left again. This will take you to Lennox Island, home of the Mi'kmaq where you can explore the history and culture at a museum, indulge in ecotourism, enjoy great walking trails or traditional Mi'kmaq dishes.

You might want to drop in to Tyne Valley Downs, one of six matinee harness racing tracks in Prince Edward Island. This training and rehabilitation centre for racehorses features the province's only matinee track exercise facility, a blacksmith shop, stalls, paddocks and of course a race track. This first class rehabilitation and training facility is part of an active harness racing industry in the province. Just watching the horses workout will give you a taste of the excitement that can be found on race night at Island tracks.

From here continue on Rte 12, diverting to Green Park Shipbuilding Museum if the urge to learn about shipbuilding, and shipbuilders takes you. This highway takes a scenic route back to Miscouche. Turn left onto Rte 2. You might want to pull into Slemon Park for a look at the successful conversion of a military base into a thriving complex housing the Atlantic Police Academy and some interesting businesses. This ends our western tour. You are back in the Summerside area after a couple of wonderful days exploring.

This tour is approximately 375 kilometers/235 miles. We seriously recommend taking 2-3 days, although you can do it in one.

Interesting to Know...Harvesting from the Sea

As you ride the western coastal region you can't help but notice the high number of heavy horses grazing in farmers fields. They are there for a very important harvest - seaweed. Locals gather up tons of Irish Moss each summer, using

horses to drag special rakes through the surf, especially after a storm. Those of you who appreciate organic and natural food will enjoy this. Harvested moss is dried by spreading on fields or wharfs, then shipped to plants where a compound called carrageenan is extracted. This is then used as a thickener in products ranging from chocolate milk to cosmetics.

In years past home cooks would use the moss to make puddings and desserts. You can enjoy a sampling of this traditional dish at the Irish Moss Café in Miminegash on the south side of the western end of the Island. Here fishermen also use boats, dragging rakes to harvest. Take time out to explore the small museum to this traditional fishery found at the Irish Moss Café.

Photo Tip: The best time to spot horses being used in the surf is after a storm. Watch near the cliffs or beaches for a worn track leading to the sea, or ask locals where to look.

Summerside

Summerside, located on Bedeque Bay offers the charms of a seaside town rich with historic and cultural influences. The city offers a host of attractions which pave the way to your enjoyment of music, theatre, spectator sports, outdoor activities, walking tours, and historic areas to explore.

photo courtesy Summerside Tourism

The waterfront is, without doubt, the hub of tourist activity. An area known as Baywalk rims the city harbour. You can cruise close by by taking Rte. 11 into the city from the east, and following Water Street. You will pass by the College of Piping and Celtic Arts where rousing performances are held regularly, before arriving at the waterfront area. Lots of parking makes it easy to access the waterside board walk. In this area you will enjoy seeing a marina, theatre, Eptek Art & Cultural Centre, sports hall of fame, the Waterfront Mall and a shopping, eating, entertainment complex known as Spinnakers' Landing - all accessed from the boardwalk. If you feel the need for liquid refreshments or a meal check out the Loyalist Inn across the street.

Turn your gaze away from land and you may just see oyster fishers "tonging" for this most succulent of shellfish, or lobster boats bringing home the catch. Recreational and working marine craft can be seen plying Summerside Harbour. The boardwalk continues, past some of the cities murals and across Confederation Trail. West of downtown on Water

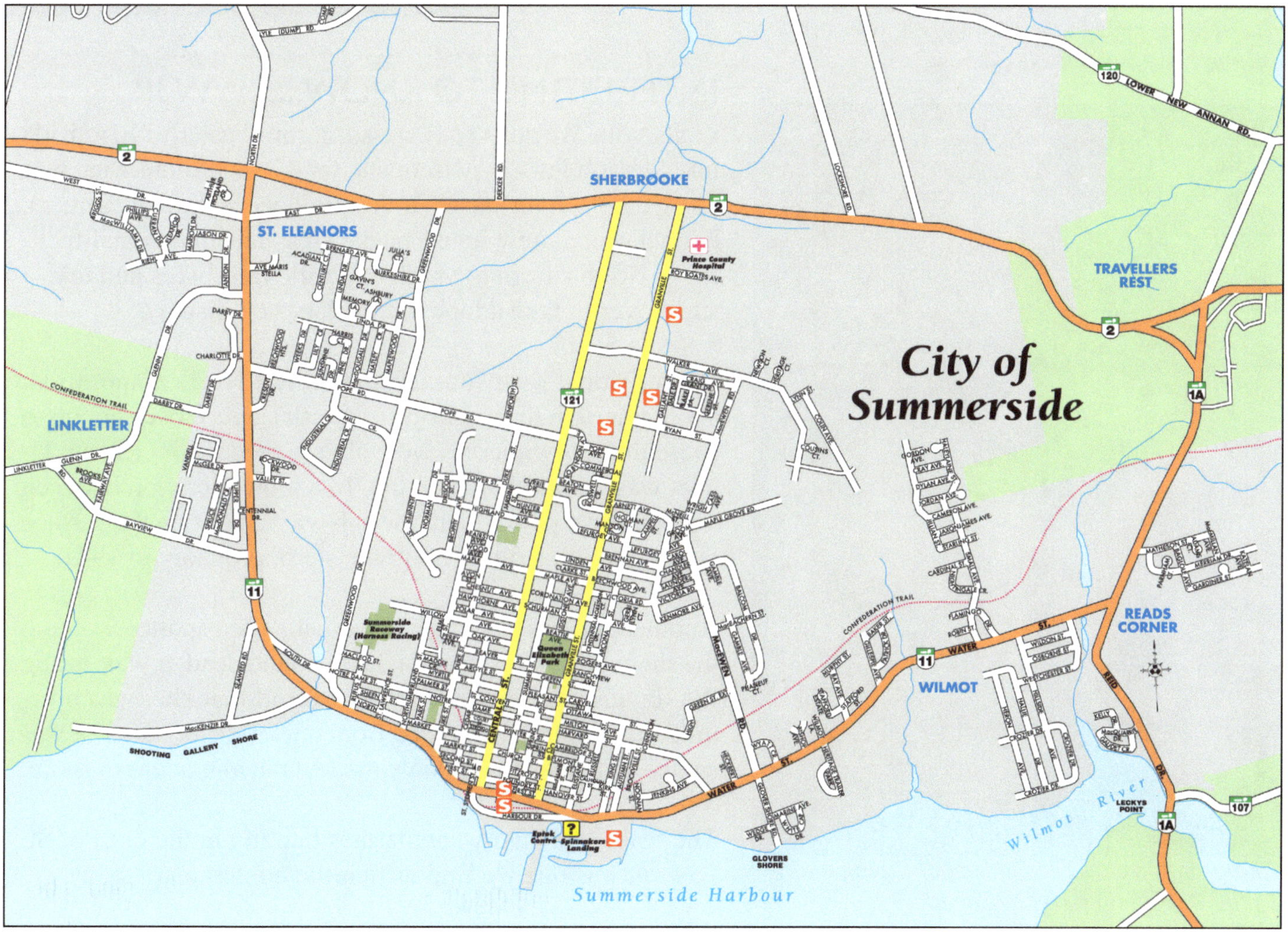

Street the site a former shipbuilding yard overlooks the harbour. It celebrates historic boat building and serves as a hub for events and entertainment. Baywalk continues west beside the beach and the harbour to Green's Shore (*photos to the right*).

Live performance rocks in this town with the heart of it all happening along Water Street. Live concerts and music events take place in various locations around the downtown core including Spinnakers Landing, Wyatt Heritage Properties and during festivals and celebrations.

For details about what is happening during your scheduled visit go to a Visitor Information Centre, as you arrive on the Island. Just a short drive from Confederation Bridge, Summerside serves as the gateway to Western Prince Edward Island which offers some spectacular riding country. It is also convenient to access touring of Central Prince Edward Island if you head east.

Guests at the Loyalist Inn have a perfect view when tall ships visit Summerside Harbout.

Photo supplied by The College of Piping and Celtic Performing Arts of Canada

Lets go Touring.....
Central
P.E.I.

Prince Edward Island National Park, overlooking Cavendish Beach.

One of the most popular Island tours takes in the area commonly referred to as the "Northshore" or "Anne's Land". Begin from either Kensington or Charlottetown and enjoy these highlights as you make the loop. (One nice thing about living on an Island, all roads eventually circle back to where you started.) We are going to go from Charlottetown.

Its an easy route to follow. First stop is at a Visitor Information Centre on Charlottetown's waterfront to pick up a map. Head out of town on Rte 15, towards Brackley Beach. Watch for the signs for the Vacationland campground. This is the site of the annual Island Rally hosted by the PEI Motorcycle Touring Club which has been hosting up to 400 visiting touring enthusiasts each year for more than 25 years. A very Telcoming campground owned and operated by motorcycling enthusiasts.

Camping at Vacationland in Brackley Beach

Worthy stops include The Dunes Studio Gallery, do check out the gardens in the back and stroll through their Gallery and shops. Visit the "Muse" at the top for a wonderful view of Brackley Bay.

Turn right onto Rte 6 - you are going to stay on Rte 6 until New London. Coming into North Rustico turn down beside Fisherman's Wharf restaurant and head down to the wharf. Follow the road right to the end, but don't go off the pavement, sand lies ahead.

Park your bike and take a stroll. There is a Fishery Museum here, you can head out in a kayak, or stroll up past the lighthouse to a breakwater and beach area. As you head back towards North Rustico village and Rte 6, there is a parking area on the water side of the road (gravel). Before you get back to the Rte 6 intersection haul over for a look at fishing boats, to book a deep sea fishing expedition, or buy lobster (cooked). Take time to chat. The folks are friendly.

Watch for signs to PEI National Park for a lovely run along the clifftops overlooking the Gulf of St. Lawrence. This ride is spectacular in the evening as the sun sets in the west. Folks gather at Cavendish to watch it set. If you wish to avoid paying the toll into the Park return to Rte 6. The roads join up in Cavendish.

Exiting the Park at Cavendish turn west, back onto Rte 6, for you are in Anne of Green Gables country, and a host of fun attractions, shops, golf courses, restaurants and such. Just keep your eyes peeled for what appeals! The Anne of Green Gables home is on your left not far from the traffic light.

Continue on Rte 6 through Stanley Bridge to New London where you turn onto Rte 20. Be prepared for more fabulous views of the bays and Gulf of St. Lawrence as you continue through French River and on to Malpeque, then Kensington. Bakin Donuts is a popular coffee stop for locals.

From the lights in Kensington you can follow Rte 2 east for a pleasant run back to Charlottetown. Or, take Rte 2 west to Summerside and as far as Tignish and North Cape.

We suggest a circular route along the south shore and back to Charlottetown. From Kensington follow Rte 2 south towards Summerside. At Traveller's Rest take Rte 1A to Rt 1 (the Trans Canada Highway), east towards Charlottetown.This region is known as the "South Shore."

There is a side trip here to Borden-Carleton, where you can view the Confederation Bridge and visit Gateway Village, great to see if you plan to arrive and leave via ferry. You won't miss seeing the engineering marvel.

The Dunes Studio Gallery and Cafe.

North Rustico Harbour is a popular end of the road stop. Here you'll enjoy watching local kids jumping from the breakwater, watching fisher folks at work, and tourists at play.

There are a number of Anne of Green Gables and Lucy Maud Montgomery sites in Cavendish and along the route as we tour the north shore. Green Gables attracts thousands each year.

Just follow the signs and turn left at the traffic lights. This street will take you down to get some awesome pictures of the bridge

Once you go through the village of Crapaud watch for the signs to Victoria. This side trip will take you to a lovely community where you can stroll on the wharf, or up through the village to find a chocolate shop, various interesting little shops, eating spots, and even a great little theatre.

The road to Victoria is a loop which takes you back to the Trans Canada. Head east again, through Desable, then turn towards the water on Rte 19. Follow this road east and enjoy the views of Northumberland Strait.

At Fort Amherst National Historic Site take time visit the interpretive centre to learn the fascinating history, walk to the site of the old fort and take in the view of Charlottetown across the harbour. A great spot in the evening, when the lights are on in the city. Sometimes a cruise ship will pass through the narrows.

Continue on Rte 19 to Cornwall where you will join the Trans Canada and continue to Charlottetown. The  distance of these two rides is about 180 km/112 mi.

Borden Lighthouse, a terrific place to photograph Confederation Bridge

Victoria-by-the-Sea lures visitors off their bikes to stroll the village streets.

Blockhouse Point Lighthouse, marks the entrance to Charlottetown Harbour. Photo taken from Fort Amherst National Historic Site looking towards Northumberland Strait

Charlottetown

Photo Tip: Cruise ships are frequent visitors to the Charlottetown waterfront, often towering over Confederation Landing Park.

As the provincial capital Charlottetown is the hub around which the Island revolves. The centre of government, it is also the entertainment capital, has the most restaurants, accommodations,and loads of shopping. The Island's largest city has combined modern amenities with the preservation of its rich history to create a premier destination.

The city has long had a reputation for welcoming visitors. Back in 1864, the Fathers of Confederation came to Charlottetown to discuss a union of the colonies. While here they were entertained, wined and dined, and had a high old time. So caught up were they with the notion of forming a country they began to hammer out the details of forming a nation in what was to become known as Canada's birthplace.

A spirit of camaraderie reigned in the town.With these grand goings on it is no wonder that Charlottetown, and indeed Prince Edward Island gained a reputation as a great place to visit. Many claim the convivial atmosphere helped along political debates that set the tone for the formation of a nation based on respect for culture and the individual citizen. Canada became a nation in 1867 but Prince Edward Island held out for a few concessions, finally joining in 1873. It remains the smallest province in Canada.

Charlottetown is still a place of celebration with festivals, theatre, sidewalk cafés, outdoor entertainment, and numerous pubs and nightspots to set your toes a-taping.

Enjoy the waterfront experience at Peake's Quay with fun eateries, entertainment, Founders Hall, marina, shops and seagoing vessels ranging from cruise ships to kayaks. Even tall ships drop by from time to time. It was here, in an area now preserved as Confederation Landing Park, that the Fathers of Confederation first came ashore.

This area of the city is steeped in heritage and history which comes alive all summer long through re-enactments, visits to Province House, Founders Hall and by walking the Olde Town where many historic buildings are restored to former glory. A continuous board walk helps you get the kinks out as it follows the shoreline to Victoria Park where a restored battery of cannon marks the spot where Yankee privateers kidnapped our Governor, back in George Washington's time.

Founders Hall, on the waterfront, is the place to learn about the birth of Canada as a nation. Also home to a large Visitor Information Centre. Cruise ships dock nearby.

The Old Town offers an abundance of eateries, bars, clubs, and shopping. Range further afield in the city for more malls and big box stores, and all services.

One of the most popular attractions on the Island, Confederation Centre of the

Arts, where Charlottetown Festival's musical productions have earned a world wide reputation, is located in the centre of downtown. The lineup is always headed by the musical Anne of Green Gables. The novel on which it is based was published more than 100 years ago. The stage production is Canada's longest running musical. The "Centre" presents other main stage shows, changing annually, free outdoor musical entertainment, and an art gallery. Check it out you may well find a production that tickles your fancy. There are several other smaller live performance venues in town, and a movie theatre that specializes in foreign and unusual films. A not to be missed performance experience is Feast Dinner Theatre at the Charlottetown Hotel. Dinner, music and laughter all wrapped up together.

Boutique shops, a touch tank with marine life, a marina, boat tours, entertainment, and eating on the upper deck are all part of a stop at Peake's Quay on the waterfront

In town you can enjoy harness racing, spectator sports, a great pool complex at the University of Prince Edward Island, movies, entertainment and more. There are two Visitor Information Centres in town, one in Founders Hall at the waterfront, and the other inside City Hall, one block from Confederation Centre. Although deemed a city Charlottetown is small when compared to large centres. With a population of around 60,000 the city is easy to get around and seldom crowded. Some of the festivals and concerts do get shoulder to shoulder but that is just how it should be.

HIDDEN TREASURES – PUBS OF OLD CHARLOTTETOWN

For Charlottetown Map see page 49

Historic olde Charlottetown, where Prince Edward Island's past is evident in architecture and historic plaques, retains an important tradition from the city's early days. Establishments which still offer the cozy warm atmosphere where warm cozy surroundings provide a place to meet and greet friends and business associates, quaff a few beverages and enjoy a good, satisfying meal.

Taverns first opened their doors in the old town almost as soon as the first settlers came ashore becoming an integral part of society and development. Indeed one, the Crossed Keys Tavern, saw many important gatherings. In 1773, Legislature met here for the first time because no other "suitable chamber" was available. The tavern's doorkeeper is said to have quipped, "This is a damned queer parliament." Queer or not, ours is the second-oldest Legislature in Canada -- only Nova Scotia's is older. It is also said that the first school was held in Cross Keys. Today's old town pubs not only preserve traditions of camaraderie and nurturing, along the way they have also preserved architecture and flavour of the past.

For Information: 1-800-955-1864 www.walkandsearchcharlottetown.com
RECOMMENDED READING - Historic Charlottetown

This piece of history sits on the Charlottetown Waterfront, in Confederation Landing Park, near where the Fathers of Confederation first landed in 1864. The replica of the bell that once rang aboard the SS Queen Victoria was presented to the City by the people of Gouldsboro, Maine. In 1866 the original bell was presented to Captain Rufus Allen of Prospect Harbour as a thank you after his brigantine, the Ponvert, and its crew from Gouldsboro rescued those aboard the SS Queen Victoria during a hurricane off Cape Hatteras. Unfortunately the 173-foot SS Queen Victoria was lost in the storm. This photo of Charlottetown's Town Crier, was taken during the unveiling of the historic artifact.

MOTORCYCLING DUO BRING FLAVOUR OF IRELAND TO CAPITAL CITY'S NIGHTLIFE & RESTAURANT SCENE

When Irish immigrant Liam Dolan spied an abandoned brick building in Charlottetown's old town it cemented his decision to make Prince Edward Island home. Liam left his native Galway Ireland with a yen to travel. Just 20 years old he left the family farm to cross the Atlantic, bound for Canada where he planned to visit his brother, before traveling on to Australia.

Like brother Tony, Liam had his chef's papers in hand when he arrived in Charlottetown. Liam's plans were put on hold when Tony had an accident. Liam took over Tony's job as a hotel chef and soon realized he had found the place he wanted to call home. He fell in love with both the Island and a local girl, named Kim. He also recognized opportunity in the need for a good seafood restaurant. Finding the heritage warehouse on Sydney Street completed a dream when he converted the space into that seafood restaurant. The Claddagh Room soon became a mainstay in the capital thanks to his culinary skills and dedication to serving the best, and freshest, the Island has to offer.

As successful as the seafood restaurant was, the Irishman was bitten by the ambition bug and looked upstairs for his next opportunity. Soon Olde Dublin Pub opened on the second floor, again retaining the wonderful atmosphere. The first establishment to be licensed as a pub this authentic Irish Pub quickly became know as a place to enjoy live entertainment, a large selection of Irish beers and draughts and true Irish pub food. Today the interior reflects the streetscape of pubs back home.

Outside their Old Dublin Pub, Liam and Kim plan the route for a relaxing run

Peakes Quay Restaurant and Bar, located beside Confederation Park on the waterfront was added when Dolan became a partner in the seasonal business. With PEI's largest outdoor patio, upstairs and overlooking the Charlottetown Harbour, Peakes is a great place to enjoy the view, good food from their pub menu and some of Atlantic Canada's best live entertainment. There are usually a number of bikes parked outside Peakes.

A true innovator Dolan spearheaded the establishment of the International Shellfish Festival held each September, fostering the links with his native Ireland through Oyster Shucking and Chowder Competitions which draw competitors from all over the world. It's all billed as an exciting, footstompin' down home kitchen party.

Liam and Kim married a year after opening Claddagh Room, now known as Claddagh Oyster House, and went on to grow both their business and their family. Two sons and three restaurants keep the Dolan family hopping. As the business got busier, the need for relaxation grew. The Dolan's found the perfect way to kick back after a busy day. They are now motorcycle enthusiasts. Kim rides a Virago 900 and Liam a Harley Davidson Ultra Classic. One of their earliest biking adventures took them to Europe for a tour; an experience that Liam says was another dream come true.

"Getting on the bike after a hard day is wonderful. The stress of running three busy restaurants just fade away. I totally relax." Of course dreams never really end. Time to tour, perhaps traveling across North America, and really enjoy exploring on their bikes are high on their agenda. "Its not always easy to get away, especially in the busy summer season, but we're working on that," he grins.

Stratford

The Town of Stratford has been a supporter of motorcycling, and Motorcycle Prince Edward Island since our beginning. In fact, the mayor, Kevin Jenkins, is an enthusiast himself and a recent Goldwing Regional Rally to be held in Prince Edward Island was based at the Stratford Town Hall.

Located just east of the capital city, the full service community is bordered to the west by the Hillsborough River and Charlottetown Harbour. To the south the waters of Northumberland Strait can be enjoyed in one of the town's parks. Tea Hill Provincial Park is a great spot to park your bike and relax at a picnic table overlooking the water, or enjoy the beach. When the tide is out there are lots of tide pools to explore. Another small park, Pondside, lies beside a small pond which is sometimes the scene of model boat competitions. Model boats and planes are popular in this community due to the presence of one of the leading model mail order business, Great Hobbies. They have a shop right here in town.

Red foxes are often spotted by golfers, proving that Fox Meadow Golf course is appropriately named.

Terry Smeltzer photos

Stratford lies at the mouth of the Hillsborough River, one of P.E.I.'s designated Canadian Heritage River systems. It offers varied experiences as you go from Charlottetown Harbour northward almost to the northshore. Home to a rich eco system, wildlife and birds abound, as does an oyster fishery. To get up close and personal to the river, take a walk in Robert L. Cotton Park, or take the tour we have outlined for you on the next page.

If you would like a day chasing a golf ball around a spectacular course look no further. The Fox Meadow Golf and Country Club championship course and the Canadian Golf Academy, a teaching facility where you can spend as little as an hour polishing your game with an expert, are right in town. Out on the main highway, you will find a large grocery store and hardware, as well as a number of other stores. Stratford also has several restaurants, a motel, campground and bed and breakfast accommodation.

Stratford is actually placed perfectly for overnighting. An equal distance from the bridge or ferry, it is just 59 km/37 mi from the Confederation Bridge to New Brunswick or 58 km/36 mi to the Wood Islands Ferry to Nova Scotia. It is also just across the bridge from Charlottetown with its theatre, nightlife, shopping and dining choices.

The Hillsborough Bridge is actually a great view point for those who slow down and take the time to look. To the south you will see the old piers from a former bridge - now home to nesting sea birds.

One tip, as you cross the bridge at night do take a careful glance at the beauty of the lights of the city or visiting ships reflecting in the harbour. During the day you may even be lucky and spot one of the cruise ships that visit each summer, or seals, cormorants and other sea birds.

Debbie Gamble photo

Let's go Touring......
The Hillsborough River

The Town of Stratford lies on the east side of the mouth of the Hillsborough River, designated a Canadian Heritage River in recognition of its significant roll in Prince Edward Island and Canadian History, as well as its importance to both the natural environment and the recreation of Islanders.

As you cross the bridge connecting Stratford to Charlottetown be aware that the waters below began their journey to empty into the Charlottetown Harbour many miles away not far from the Island's north shore.

It is from this bridge that we will take you on a tour that starts in Stratford and follows the river north for a ride you can enjoy as a short run, or extend to include one of the Province's premier attractions, Greenwich.

Head west from Stratford, across the Hillsborough Bridge which is located on Rte 1. As you come off the bridge, turn right (at the first traffic lights). Follow this road (bypass) to Rte 2. You will pass by the provinces largest hospital on the right.

At Rte 2, or St. Peters Road, turn right towards Mount Stewart a distance of about 30 km/19 mi. You will notice several "Heritage River" signs which you can follow to the shoreline, and a pull off near Scotchford which provides a great view and information signage. Caution: Many of these roads turn to clay which can be heavily rutted, and slippery in rain.

About 4 km/2 1/2 mi down the road turn right to Mount Stewart and drop in to the Hillborough River Eco-Centre to learn about the eagles and other wildlife that inhabit the area as well as the history and natural diversity. The folks here will direct you to several nature trails that provide great walking and photography experiences.This is the home of the annual Hillsborough River Eagle Festival held in the spring. Within the village you can enjoy a meal or coffee stop.

Now its decision time. For a short version of our tour, continue through the village, then follow Rte 22, to Rte 21, turn right and follow it back into Stratford. A distance of about 30 km/19 mi.

Or, if you are ready for more riding, return to Rte 2, and turn right. This will take you northeast towards Morell. Just a couple of km down the road stop in at St. Andrews Chapel and the Bishop McEachern National Historic Site. Just a few years ago The Friends of St. Andrews accomplished an amazing feat.

St. Andrews Chapel

They moved the burned out shell of Prince Edward Island's first college chapel from Charlottetown back to its original home here at St. Andrews. Over 100 years earlier the chapel was moved by dozens of horses down the frozen river to Charlottetown. Restored it is a cherished heritage building, host to lectures and concerts. Looking towards the river you can see a pioneer French and Scottish cemetary where a Celtic Cross honours early Scots.

As you continue east, passing through Morell you soon find yourself riding beside St Peters Bay. St. Peters village is a good stop for a break - do check out the Pewter shop. Then follow the signs to Greenwich in the Prince Edward Island National Park. Here you can learn about the dune systems and this unique part of the world at the interpretive centre, walk amazing trails, swim, or just savour the beauty. To return retrace your ride to Stratford. This trip fits well into a half day, or longer if you explore.

HILLSBOROUGH RIVER

In the earliest days of human habitation, the Mi'kmaq camped along the shores of the river they knew as Mimtugaak. They paddled its waters and fished or harvested shellfish and many still reside in the area near Scotchfort.

By the early 18th century Europeans saw the value of the river, one of three that empties into Charlottetown Harbour which was protected by the French at Port La Joie until it was taken by the British and became Fort Amherst. It was valued by hunters and as one of few "highways" into the interior. Remnants of Acadian dykes are proof of early French settlement. As communities were established the river quickly became important to the ship building industry that was vital to the development of the colony.

Today the river plays an equally vital role in the preservation of the natural environment. For visitors nature appreciation possibilities include viewing sites such as the Glenfinnan Island Great Blue Heron colony; watching bald eagle and osprey fishing; and bird watching on overland trails. The estuary supports a variety of shellfish and finfish; brook and rainbow trout and occasionally striped bass are popular with anglers. Hunting for waterfowl is outstanding in the watershed, especially within the nominated area. The floodplain landscape features estuaries, fresh water lakes and ponds and provides excellent feeding and migrating grounds for various species. Blue-winged teal and brant join black ducks and Canada geese are the most common.

Occasionally unusual sightings appear in the river. Several years ago a large shark reportedly made its way up to Mount Stewart. Our photographer, just beginning his career, was sent out by the newspaper to try for pictures accompanied by his mom, now your publisher. We never did find the shark, but we did discover the many roads that lead to the river, the abundance of nature to be enjoyed and the beauty of the region.

As you travel parallel to the river follow the Heritage River symbols for a closer look. Some of these turn to clay, and probably rutted roads, be careful. Recreational activities include: birdwatching, fishing, bicycling (rentals in Mt. Stewart), walking and hiking along nature trails. Canoe & kayak excursions are available out of Charlottetown. Inquire at the Visitor Information Centre for guided tours or Mount Stewart's Interpretive Centre.

The Hillsborough is alive with human heritage appreciation opportunities. There are festivals and events, musical evenings, museums and sites of cultural importance.

Let's go touring......

Eastern PEI

The folks in Eastern Prince Edward Island wisely suggest that one engage all of the senses when visiting their area. See the sheer beauty - the line of cultivated fields stretching to cliff edges, unexpected forests, white farmhouses with laundry blowing in the breeze, a tantalizing stretch of red dirt road leading to a country destination, the clear blue waters of Northumberland Strait and picturesque fishing harbours.

Listen for the steady drone of fishing boats traveling effortlessly out to sea, the lap of waves breaking on the sand, birds calling as they wheel overhead. Smell wild rose bushes mingled with the salt air. Eastern Prince Edward Island is a relatively undiscovered special place. Feel the singing sands beneath your feet, the sea-mist on your face during an early morning or after-dusk ride, or the joy of a camera in hand as you take a boat tour to seal or heron colonies. You can even taste the special flavours found at the Island's only winery and distilleries!

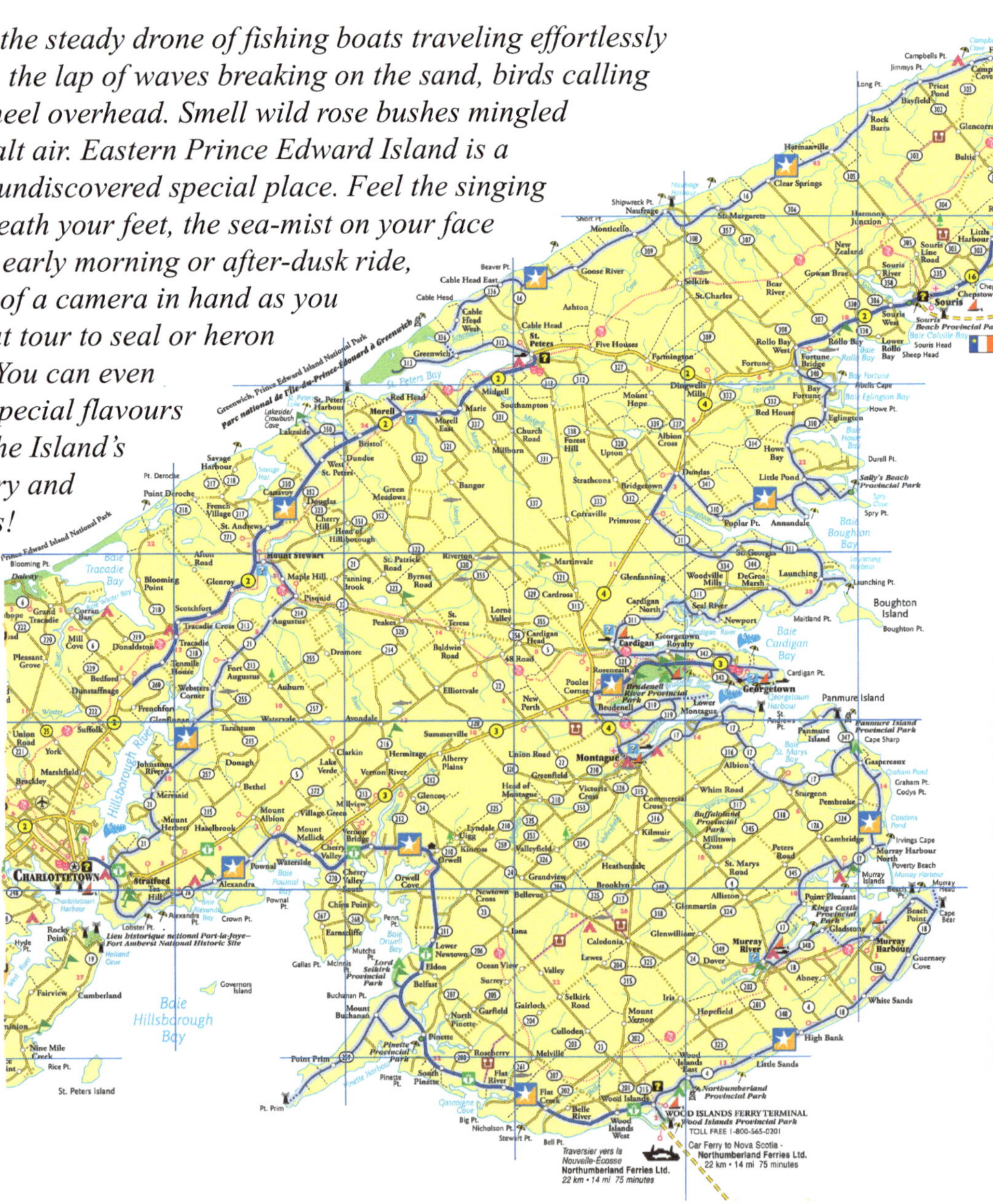

Montague
watefront

A riding tour of eastern Prince Edward Island will encompass friendly communities, breathtaking lookouts, endless beaches, distinctive lighthouses, provincial parks, heritage roads and much more.

If you are the type of person who likes to follow a pre-plotted route then you will love the colourful starfish signs which make it easy to discover special places when exploring the Points East Coastal Drive. This route is marked on provincial maps with the starfish symbol and is a wonderful loop tour.

There are loads of sideroads and alternate routes to explore - just take out your map to set off on your own adventure. For now we'll follow the Points East tour.

This is a route that can very easily be given two or three days. There any many points where you can spend a full day. Absolutely fabulous beaches, for instance, at Panmure Island, Basin Head and Greenwich, and lots of smaller, more intimate beaches along the way can keep sun lovers enthralled for a full day all on their own.

Now you are going to need a start point. Logically that will be Charlottetown or Wood Island - one of the two Island entry points. Since our last tour ended in Stratford, located to the east of Charlottetown, this seems a logical place to start. Heading east on Rte 1, toward Wood Islands you will soon spot the starfish signs.

At Orwell, those who enjoy a look back at the past should turn left to Orwell Corner Historic Village. Its well signed. It is a great place to look at agriculture and a country crossroads community in the 1890s. Just up the road Sir Andrew MacPhail Homestead National Historic Site is another great stop, with a restored home where you can enjoy refreshments or a meal, some walking trails, gardens and exhibits.

Orwell Corner hosted the first annual URGAT (Ural Gathering) on grounds of the Historic Village. Side car rigs were parked in the Village school yard where site visitors were invited to take a look see.

Back on Rte 1 watch for signs to Lord Selkirk Park, with its Scottish culture centre and to Point Prim. Side road, Rte 209, ends at the Point Prim lighthouse.

As you enter Wood Islands you pass a Visitor Information Centre where you can pick up a guide to the region, check on special events and even shop. If you carry on down the highway following the signs to the ferry , bear left just before the toll booths and follow the road around to the Wood Island Provincial Park. This is a great spot for photos of fishing boats, the ferry and birds in the shallow waters on both sides of the ferry terminal. There is a beach , and don't miss visiting the Wood Islands Lighthouse and Museum.

To continue, go back to the Visitor Information Centre, pick up Rte 4 East, then Rte 18. In Little Sands you will pass by the Island's first winery. Rossignol Estate Winery offers a wonderful photo stop, winery to visit and an art gallery.

It's a beautiful drive to Cape Bear Lighthouse and Marconi Museum. It is said that the first distress calls from the Titanic were picked up here. Keep going through Murray Harbour, Murray River and on to Murray Harbour North. The starfish symbols mark the way. You can go seal watching out of Murray River or for Birding Tours out of Murray Harbour, check out the beach at Murray Harbour North, or Panmure Island.

By now you may well have wiled away a day. Overnight along the way or in nearby Montague. Located on one of our Canadian Heritage Rivers. More information about Montague on the following pages. The Three Rivers area of Brudenell, Cardigan and Montague is home to the most recently designated Canadian Heritage River system in P.E.I. The rich cultural history is evident at Brudenell Point, the site of an early French settlement now known as Roma at Three Rivers.

Just a little further on the community of Georgetown offers a beautiful perspective of two of the rivers. In fact you can enjoy a great meal, visit the interpretive centre, and even visit Kings County Playhouse, one of the oldest theatres in Canada where some wonderful performances can be enjoyed in an intimate setting.

Coming and going you will pass by Brudenell River Provincial Park. Drive in - you'll be amazed at the diverse opportunities to enjoy the great outdoors that are here.

As you continue north east you will pass by the Inn at Bay Fortune, the home of a television program The Inn Chef, which launched the television career of Chef Michael Smith, who is now the star of several cooking/food shows on the Food Television Network.

Rollo Bay is known for its music. The ferry to Isle de la Madeleine draws people to Souris and they have a great beach right on the side of the road as you come into town.

Continuing north east takes you to one of the showcase beaches of P.E.I., at Basin Head. Here the sand sings to the delight of many visitors. The beach is accessed by way of a great fisheries museum. Take time out to develop a real appreciation for the life of those who work in our inshore fishery. Basin Head is a place where you can easily wile away a day, especially if you love the beach.

The final leg of our easterly trek takes us to East Point Lighthouse. After a visit (see the Lighthouse Tour for more info) you will now turn west, still on Rte. 16.

North Lake is home to a thriving deep-sea fishing industry. Not only to they land the mighty bluefin tuna, but the fortunate may even see whales or seals during their trip. This port is a photographer's dream.

Georgetown

Basin Head

North Lake

If you have any train buffs in your group a side trip to Elmira will reveal a museum dedicated to P.E.I.'s railway, the PEI Miniature Railway and Atlantic Canada's largest model train collection. The restored station marks the end of the line for the railway, which has been transformed into one of our proudest attractions, Confederation Trail, a linear park.

The windmills in this area are a reminder of Prince Edward Island's commitment to being an energy concious province.

Back in the saddle, continue west. You can drop in to tour the Prince Edward Island Distillery in Hermanville where PEI potatoes become a premium Vodka. Then it's a short run to Greenwich, the eastern most portion of the PEI National Park. If you feel like a walk try the floating boardwalk, it takes you up close to a delicate dune system and beautiful white sand beaches. It's a good idea to visit the Interpretive Centre to learn about Greenwich, and the natural history of this wonderful area before exploring the trails. Doubles ones appreciation.

Back in St. Peters, pick up Rte 2 west, towards Charlottetown. This area, and the trip back is included in the Hillsborough River Tour. Visit the Capital city, or follow road signs to Stratford.

East Point

Elmira

Before heading out to discover the 475 km/295 mi of Points East Coastal Drive, you can pick up a touring map and a Rally Tour Guide which breaks it down into 8 Discovery Drives and outlines 105 points of interest along the entire route. The Guide is available as a PDF document online at www.pointseast-coastaldrive.com or from tourist information locations, stores and accommodations along Points East Coastal Drive.

The small town of Georgetown is home to a fine small theatre known as Kings Playhouse.

BIKER ACTIVITIES

Rallies, rides and other special events are planned by a number of clubs and organizations. To check out what is happening during your visit go to

www.motorcyclepei.com

and click on "Events Calendar'. Or, contact the clubs listed on page 37. Keep in mind that executives and contacts can change, so check 'Club Listings' on the same website or go to club's sites.

Events held by the motorcycle community begin each year with a spring motorcycle show, a great chance to meet and greet, as well as oooh and ahhhh over the latest and greatest offerings on display by dealers. Rallies and rides tend to vary according to national club schedules and the focus of current club executives. There are several annual events as well as new ones being added every year.

Montague

At midpoint on your eastern tour you will enter Montague, one of those small towns where you need to slow down to cruisin' speed, put up your visor and just enjoy the tranquil atmosphere, the treelined streets, heritage homes, a heritage river and pristine waterfront. Small town friendly; a terrific stop.

Montague is the largest community in Eastern PEI. Whether you want to fill your tank, with a meal or refreshment, your bike's with gas, or just need a break, you will find the amenities and services you need. Stock up on groceries, visit the liquor store or the bank.

Feel like stretching your legs? Down by the waterfront bordering the serene Montague River you will find parking near the former train station. Its easy to find as its beside the only bridge on this stretch of highwy. You can take a walk along the picturesque Confederation Trail which borders the serene river to the east of the station or just enjoy the parkland. There is a great place to partake of refreshment down at water level at the station. There are a number of wood carvings here one of them a not-very-attractive mermaid. She keeps an eye on the activity at the marina which is home to fishing, recreational and tour boats. You can board a river cruise to view the landscape and wildlife from the water. A great chance to kick back with no need to keep your eye on the road.

You may see seals and will see some of the 333 species of birds known to visit the region. Some of the most spectacular sightings will take place on a river cruise available from the Marina easily seen from the bridge over Montague River.

If history tickles your fancy, drop in to the Garden of the Gulf Museum. Its the large brick building across the river from the old station and river front, located on the east side as you come off the bridge. Some of us can spent hours pouring over their collection. Ask about special events at the museum.

Great little information centre in the former station. They will happily direct you to some of the not-to-be-missed spots in the area:
- The historic town of Georgetown with a great little theatre
- Picturesque Cardigan
- Beautiful Panmure Island
- the historic site, Roma at Three Rivers, a reconstruction of the first commercial settlement of PEI found at Brudenell Point.

You are in a region of rolling hills, meandering rivers, lush forests, scenic lighthouses, tempting beaches, wooded areas and a lush agricultural lands. If you follow the eastern tour you will pass through this great little town and miles of scenic roads. For more information about Montague and events go to www.montaguepei.com

Clubs

For many of us the best part of the motorcycling life is the social side. The chance to spend time with like minded folk, trade tales of rides enjoyed, roads explored, people met. Clubs or organizations devoted to this lifestyle we love are the best places to do that.

There are a number of active groups in Prince Edward Island with different mandates, goals and guidelines. We have listed a number of organizations below. The best way to find out more about them, and whats going on during your visit is to contact them for details.

PEI MOTORCYCLE TOURING CLUB

Active for over 25 years, the PEIMTC was formed to develop and promote safety, friendship, good will, and a favourable image with the general public, both on and off-Island. This family-oriented club holds summer rides, and during winter enjoy movie or games nights, sleigh rides, and Sunday get-to-gethers.

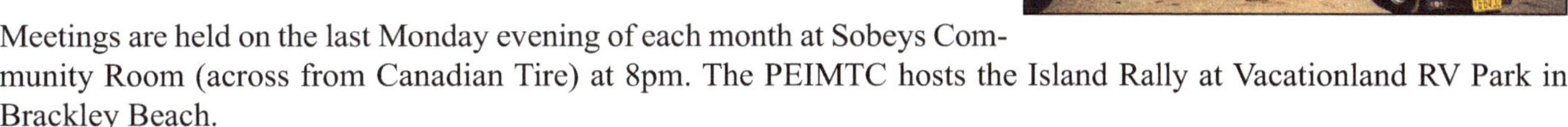

Membership is open to anyone age 19 or over, who is a motorcycle rider, or is a motorcycle enthusiast. The club's official charity is a fund designed to assist with the costs incurred by individuals (and their families) needing medical care out of province.

Meetings are held on the last Monday evening of each month at Sobeys Community Room (across from Canadian Tire) at 8pm. The PEIMTC hosts the Island Rally at Vacationland RV Park in Brackley Beach.

For more info: p/f Sharon at (902) 629-1320, or Fax # (902) 629-1319 or write PEIMTC, P.O. Box 2856, Charlottetown, PEI C1A 8C4; email (underthesun@pei.sympatico.ca) or log on to (http://www.angelfire.com/pe/peimtc). Rally dates August 27 - 29, 2010 for Island Rally. (www.redislandrun.com)

GWRRA CHAPTER "A" PEI

"FRIENDS FOR FUN, SAFETY AND KNOWLEDGE." - Gold Wing Road Riders Association stands for an atmosphere of fun, safety, and knowledge to Gold Wing and Valkyrie motorcycle owners, as well as non-Gold Wing owners. The Association provides a culture which fosters shared values, team concepts and camaraderie.

Chapter "A" PEI meets the 3rd Sunday of every month, 1 pm at the Stratford Town Hall, 234 Shakespear Drive in Stratford. Activities include their Tour Master program, which visits interesting points across PEI, riding skills program, as well as BBQ's, Poker runs, corn boil camp out, bowling, sleigh rides, coffee get-togethers, Christmas party, etc. Rides scheduled monthly. For more info: Stephen and Cornelia Pineau, pineausgoldwing@gmail.com, or www.chapterapei.web.com

PEI HARLEY OWNERS GROUP (HOG)

The PEI chapter of the Harley Owners Group is under the sponsorship of Red Rock Harley-Davidson. The Chapter has been active in raising funds and providing toys for kids in need for most of its existence. Members participate in many different runs raising thousands of dollars for various children's charities including Camp Gencheff and Children's Wish Foundation

The Chapter plans a safe and exciting season of riding and social events (all makes welcome on Chapter rides.) Their weekly pick-up rides are open to anyone who loves to ride motorcycles. Meetings are held on the 1st Monday of each month. For more info: check the bulletin board in the H.O.G. room at Red Rock Harley-Davidson on the Warren Grove Road in North River. www.peihog.com

CANADIAN MOTORCYCLE CRUISERS

CMC is an 100% all Canadian, family oriented riding club with chapters in every province and four chapters (with 130 members) on PEI. CMC welcomes both new and veteran riders, on all makes and models, with special attention placed on rider safety, and enjoyment of the biking lifestyle. There are no membership fees to join.

They hold weekly and monthly rides, with experienced road captains. Rides held bi-weekly. Leaving Tim Hortons, 385 Grafton Street, Charlottetown or Tim Hortons, 820 Water Street every Tuesday at 7 pm and Sundays at 1 pm. More info: cmcsummerside@hotmail.com, or www.cmcpei.ca

RED KNIGHTS PEI CHAPTER 1

Red Knights is an international motorcycle club for members of the fire service, and their families, who enjoy riding motorcycles. Membership is open to ALL firefighters, active or retired, volunteer, or industrial, who have access to a motorcycle and hold a valid motorcycle drivers license. Spouses, members' children, boy/girlfriends and brothers/sister can be Social Members. To start a new chapter, a minimum of 7 firefighter members is required. Red Knights take part in the nation-wide campaign Fire Fighters supporting Muscular Dystrophy Canada - Let's Make Muscles Move, since 1954. Rides are Thursday evenings at 7 pm, leaving the Charlottetown Fire Department Station 2, 152 St. Peters Road. For more info, contact Scott Ryan, President at sryan@city.charlottetown.pe.ca or surf to www.redknightsmc.com

CANADIAN ARMY VETERANS (CAV) www.thecav.ca

South Africa Unit & Misano Ridge Unit (2nd CAV)

Under the name of Canadian Army Veterans The CAV is a brotherhood of serving and veteran motorcycle enthusiasts who have volunteered to serve our country, whether it be in regiments, on ships or with air squadrons or bases across Canada and overseas. CAV units formed across Canada are named in tribute of Canadian Battle Honours, to continue the traditions and bonds formed in war and peace. The CAV was formed by Canadian Veterans whose common bond was service to one's country and the fact they were avid motorcyclists. To date we have members who have served our country in every theatre of military operations, in peace or at war; as members of NATO, the United Nations or members of Canada s present Army, Navy or Air Force.

Our Mission is to provide our members with a unit to continue service to each other and our communities and country. We are a brotherhood of Canadian Army Veterans, mounted on motorcycles of all different types. The CAV promotes safe, responsible motorcycling. Alongside our Veteran Supporter members, (brothers, sisters, husbands, wives, partners, friends and comrades that share a love of country, community and motorcycles) we continue to volunteer our time for our Country by actively supporting each other, our brothers in arms and our communities through charity rides and events.

The CAV is now represented on PEI by the South Africa Unit located in Charlottetown & Misano Ridge Unit located in Summerside. South Africa Unit (Charlottetown) don t have regular meetings at present but are in the planning stages for the upcoming riding season, with a charity ride planned Ride for the Troops in July. Contact South Africa Unit by email 2CAVSouthAfrica@thecav.ca

CHRISTIAN MOTORCYCLISTS ASSOCIATION

Prince Edward Island members of this group of men and women who love motorcycling and love Jesus offer assistance to those in need. They also organize the PEI Biker Blessing, in 2010 in conjunction with Canada's Motorcycle Ride For Dad raising money to fight prostate cancer through research and awareness.. For five years they have been holding an annual Run for the Son. The group put donations to good use, sending bibles to 'restructed access' countries through Open Door Ministries, Motorcycles for Native Pastors through Missionary Ventures and Outreach to Canadian motorcyclists through the Christian Motorcyclists Association of Canada. Local contacts: Blair & Janet Neill: (Area Rep.) underthesun@pei.sympatico.ca 902 672-1933, Lance & Carla Inman 902 888-8715, Ron & Coleen Arsenault 902-888-2245

TIGNISH BIKERS

Tignish Bikers are an informal small group of enthusiasts with a love of getting together to ride. For more information on the Tignish Bikers, contact Christa Gaudet at 882-3668 or gaudetchrista@hotmail.com

PEI MOTOCROSS

Fans of Motocross racing need not fear going into withdrawal whilst on PEI - thanks to the PEI Motorcross line-up of events! Get your fill of "Big Air" at one of the Island tracks: the PEI Mudrooters track in Desable (just off the Appin Rd, directly across from the Car Life Museum), or the West Prince Motocross track on the Duvar Road near Mill River or Burkes MX Park at Rollo Bay (on the main highway, on the left as you are going toward Souris. Formed to promote recognition and growth of motocross on PEI, they see MX as very much a family-oriented sport, and the group encourages family admittance.

For more information, visit: www.imxc.ca, or email peimudrooters@gmail.com For details about race days, www.motorcyclepei.com and click on Events.

Iron-butt enthusiasts from British Columbia made a fast run to the Island Rally hosted by the PEI Motorcycle Touring Club.

British Car Days attract enthusiasts of 2 and 4 wheel vehicles from across North America

Sterling Page of Sunset Beach, North Carolina and John Kendall of Grafton, Massachusets heard about the Atlantic Canada European Motorcycle Weekend held at the Silver Fox Yacht and Curling Club in Summerside and the Lobster Carnival. John, sporting a gold "Bum Burner " achievement on his plate holder, and his travelling buddy were on the ride of a lifetime. Heading to Newfoundland via Cape Breton's Sydney ferry, they planned a circular trip to Happy Valley Labrador, and then through the only recently opened road to Quebec.

Things to do... just a few ideas

BOOKS AND BOOKSELLERS - Sellers of new books are to be found in Charlottetown and Summerside. If you are a collector of the rare, unusual or antique books then there are a number of antiquarian and second hand sellers to be found in the brochure Booksellers of Atlantic Canada. Check www.seacroftpei.com for a selection of local books.

BIRDWATCHING - Opportunities are great for catching a glimpse of birds, especially during spring and fall migration periods. Many pass across the Island on their way north to breed, then, like human snowbirds, they head south for the winter months. During these periods it is possible to see as many as a hundred different species in a day. Some areas boast as many as 333 different birds spotted during a year. Among them are many sea birds, most noticeably Cormorants, Ducks, Canada Geese, Eiders, and Scooters, along with seagulls and such.

CRAFTS AND ARTISANS - A passionate and vibrant craft industry provides many opportunities to view wonderful creations, meet creative artisans and shop. Its great to incorporate a visit to artists, craft producers, or the shops that feature their wares into your touring. To make that easier the government produces a free Prince Edward Island Craft, Art and Giftware Directory which can be picked up at any Visitor Information Centre. This booklet tells you who is doing what, who offers tours or special activities, hours of operation and has a map. A Studio Tour held in late September is a great way to tour - seeking out chosen artisans is grand fun.

GOLF - There are 30+ golf opportunities in this small province with courses to suit all levels of play never more than a short ride away. Three courses rank in Canada's top 100. A golfing school can improve your play. Green fees are considered a bargain in the world of golfers. Many courses offer club rentals, and several resorts have packages that include accommodation and green fees. Check it all out by contacting Golf Prince Edward Island Canada at: 1-866-GOLF-PEI (465-3734) or www.golfpei.ca

HIKING, WALKING - Dozens of trails and walking paths can be found in PEI ranging from short trails in communities or parks, to the grandaddy of them all Confederation Trail built along the corridors of the former railroad. The tip-to-tip route from Tignish to Elmira offers 270 km/168mi of trail. Add in branch trails and you have 400 km/248 mi to choose from. Easily accessed where they cross roads, they provide a great place to stretch your legs and bond with nature. The trail is marked on the provincial map provided at Visitor Information Centres. Watch for plum-coloured gates marking entry points. Several stations are still in use, some as interpretive centres delving into history. Trails take you into wetlands, hardwood forests, beside waterways and through farmlands. Great for nature lovers, artists, photographers and more. Depending on the season you will see mayflowers, berries to savour, apples to crunch. You might even be lucky enough to cross streams black with fish in the spring. There are even more trails, board walks and groomed paths to choose from, especially in the PEI National Park, Provincial Parks, coastal communities, Charlottetown and Summerside. .

HORSE RACING - the excitement of live harness racing can be enjoyed at several tracks including Charlottetown, Summerside. The Charlottetown Driving Park offers seasonal racing and betting at major standardbred and thoroughbred centres and a gaming facility. To really experience the appeal that these trotting or pacing horses driven from a sulky have, go to the smaller community tracks.

MUSEUMS - Thirty-nine Community Museums provide special places to delve into history. They range from lighthouses containing collections about shipping, lighthouse keepers, shipwrecks and marine history; to the birthplace of Anne of Green Gables, to Shellfish Museums, Agricultural Museums and even foxes and basket weavers. For a full listing of Museums visit a Visitor Information Centre. Watch for them when touring - great places to take a break.

WRITING - Our most famous author, Lucy Maud Montgomery, introduced Prince Edward Island to the world more than 100 years ago when her first novel, Anne of Green Gables was published. Lucy Maud sent a message to the world that this is a great place to write, and to write about. Her tradition is picked up by the Island Writers Association whose mandate is to educate, inform and encourage writing. They offer workshops periodically throughout the year which are designed to be both a great way to spend a day and an opportunity to learn more about writing and publishing at both a hobby and professional level. For information go to www.seacroftpei.com/writers

This small Island can surprise those who seek new challenges and experiences in the great outdoors:

BY LAND	BY SEA
beachcombing	canoeing
bicycling	cruises
bird watching	deep-sea fishing
camping	diving
cycling	ecotourism
golf	freshwater fishing
horseback riding	kayaking
hunting	parasailing
harness racing	sail boat charters
rallying	seal watching
tennis	swimming
touring	windsurfing
walking & hiking	

North Rustico

ENJOYING THE GREAT OUTDOORS

Camping and picnicing take a little extra planning and work, but for many folk are an integral part of touring by bike. Staying at a campground like Vacationland in Brackley Beach, which is owned by biking enthusiast, Tom Nicholls is a sure way to ensure a warm welcome. Vacationland hosts the annual Island Rally hosted by the PEI Motorcycle Touring Club.

VACATIONLAND RV PARK
BRACKLEY BEACH, PEI
www.vacationlandrv.ca

Adding something good to eat to your outdoor experience can be as simple as roasting marshmellows over a campfire, or a more complex lobster boil, complete with corn on the cob, potatoes and mussels.

The challenge is the pot. Luckily some tourism operators will either organize such a feast, or help you with the pot. The seafood is best obtained from a fishing wharf, and cooked in heavily salted water or clean seawater.

Of course an easier alternative is to pick up take out picnic fare. Any way you do it, dining outdoors is relaxing and a fun part of any vacation.

WOOD ISLANDS LIGHTHOUSE

The lighthouse located in the park just east of the ferry terminal and fishing wharfs is one of Prince Edward Island's hidden treasurers. Described as a museum and gift shop, the site offers much, much more than one would expect.

A daily "Taste Our History Program" provides guests with the opportunity to sample foods of yesterday from Gramma's old cookbooks - examples are bannock, homemade jams and jellies, cornmeal bread, ginger cookies, chocolate potato cake, dulce etc. Something different is offered each day. Delicious bake sales take place at various times throughout the summer.

In mid-July they host an annual "Sea Glass Festival." The second annual event will take place in 2010. More info available on the Sea Glass site at peiseaglassfestival.com. The first Sea Glass Festival was a huge success. Organizers are "very excited with all the interest and excitement both from the Island and away.

Moonlight Tours take place in July and August, one per month with refreshments, entertainment, guided tours amid lantern lit rooms, etc. One of their favorite events.

Daily tours are offered at the Lighthouse or you may also go exploring on your own. The lighthouse has 11 themed rooms full of area history and culture including the Rum-Running Room, Burning/Phantom Ship Room, Interpretive Room for Island Lighthouses, Fisheries Room, Lightkeeper's Quarters, etc. They also feature inter-actives and videos, to aid in your experience. "We are pleased to be able to provide French speaking visitors with our written tour in French to enhance their lighthouse experience.

In 2009 the folks in charge upped and moved the lighthouse a few hundred feet away from the cliffs, which were eroding dangerously close to the structure. Quite a feat!Open: June 13-Sept 11, 2010 daily 9:30-6pm, last admission ticket sold at 5:30pm
www.woodislandslighthouse.com

photo provided by Wood Island Lighthouse

INTRODUCING – THE FOLKS BEHIND THE LIGHT

Back in 1998 a group known as "Keepers of the Light" decided to dust off the old lighthouse and open it to the public. The results reflect the many hours spent preserving the structure and the fact that this on going project is a labour of love for all involved. Heather MacMillan, Nancy Perkins and Don Wheeler were part of the initial committee and are now joined by Kris Rollins, secretary and Bev Stewart, summer supervisor. Kris and Nancy head up a Sea Glass Festival held in mid-July. The first Sea Glass Festival was a huge success and this one is shaping up to be even bigger and better.

"Our 'Friendship Garden' that was started by our last lightkeeper, Leon Patton was unfortunately desgtroyed when our lighthouse was relocated from the edge of the bank further inland to safer ground. Fortunately, we were abel to save some of Leon's lilies to begin a new garden. Our beautiful rose bushes were planted by the second last lightkeeper, George Stewart," says Heather. "I make rosehip syrup from them in the spring to sell in our Captain Angus Brown giftshop at the Lighthouse. Everything around us down there has special meaning and we try to open it up for the community and our visitors to experience and enjoy in a fun and educational way."

School groups from Pictou come each June as their annual trip. "Bev has put together a wonderful activity book for each student and I treat them with homemade chocolate chip cookies. They have a wonderful day with us and crossing on the ferry to get to us is a treat as well."

Its all part of the community spirit that makes this a great spot to visit.

Photos to be proud of ...the perfect souvenier

One of the best things to happen to those who enjoy motorcycle touring is the development of the digital camera. Now it is possible to record your vacation and to take great photos featuring your bike using a small compact camera that fits in a pocket or fanny pack. Recognizing that photography is a great way to have souvenirs of your trip we asked professional photographer John C. Watson of Imagemaker Photographic Studio to share some tips for getting good photos.

by John C. Watson

Motorcycles provide their owners with many hours of enjoyment and are often considered their "pride and joy". Including your bike in vacation photos ensures wonderful memories, and great bragging rights!

I've often been asked about the best way to photograph motorcycles. Many people are disappointed that they were not able to show the bike at it's best or are dissatisfied with the photos of their touring adventures. The following simple tips and tricks will produce much more pleasing results if you take the time to think about them before "snapping" a photo. While these are written with a focus on the bike, the same guidelines apply to your scenics.

PAY ATTENTION TO LIGHT

The first thing to be aware of is how your bike is being lit. Usually it is being lit by the sun so one must pay attention to where the sun is in relation to the bike. The best time for photography is before 10:30 am and after 2 pm. During the midday hours the sun is directly above the earth and produces the least flattering light. In the hours before and after midday the light is hitting the landscape at an angle which creates shadow and depth as well as bringing out rich colours in a scene.

The further away you are from noon the more dramatic the lighting. That's why sunrises and sunsets are so beautiful. So if possible try not to shoot in the midday sun. A trick to use is to think of a clock. As you stand looking at your bike, at "12", and you are at "6" try and keep the sun between "3" and "9" and you will always have nice lighting on your bike. Watch for your own shadow and make sure it isn't creeping into your picture anywhere, especially on the ground in front of you or even creeping up and falling onto your bike.

If you want to make sure you can see lots of detail, especially in around the engine, move your bike into the shade or wait for the sun to go behind a cloud. When you can't see any shadows on the ground you know you will be able to see the most detail. This actually creates more even light on the bike allowing the hidden areas of the engine to be more easily seen.

We have included numerous photo tips in the guide, which point out great locations to get great shots!

Coastal villages, Confederation Bridge, the ferries and typical Island structures like lighthouses and historic buildings are great backdrops for 'placing' your photos.

CHANGE YOUR ANGLE

Cape Tryon

Don't be afraid to change your angle. Most often people take photos from a normal standing position. Experiment a little, try getting low to the ground and shooting up at your bike. Get up a little higher and show more of the top of the bike. Move side to side as well, sometimes just changing your position can make for a greatly improved photo. Moving further away from your bike allows you to get more of the scene around you showing all the wonderful places you've been on your road trips and the places your bike has taken you. If you want to feature just your bike then try moving in closer to fill the viewfinder with just the bike. Make sure to take note of any guidelines that may be seen in your viewfinder as these tell you what area of the viewfinder will actually show in your photos. Move in even closer to show detailed paint jobs or other special features but not to close! Most point and shoot type cameras need to be at least 3 feet away from a subject in order to focus. Check your owner's manual to find out how close you can be to your subject.

TAKE TIME TO COMPOSE / "THE RULE OF 3RD'S"

One of the other most common habits is to place the subject of the photo (your bike) in the very center of the picture. One trick I use is called the "Rule of 3rd's". As you look through the viewfinder of your camera divide the scene into an imaginary tic-tac-toe grid. When photographing your bike in a scene place your bike at the points where the lines intersect. This is more pleasing to the eye, makes the shot more dynamic and shows the surrounding scene. If you want to fill the photo mostly with the bike place the middle of the tires along the bottom horizontal line and you will always have a well-balanced photo.

Taking the time to decide exactly what elements you want to see in your photo, and making sure they are where you want them to be, is easier than trying to fix something later. Leaving a bit more room than is actually needed will allow for more cropping options later on. The standard camera format of 4x6 (which equates to 8x12) must have enough "extra room" if you want to produce an 8x10 inch print. Basically you will loose 2 inches off the longest side - either all from one end or 1 inch from both ends. If the photo was taken too close to the subject you may be required to cut off important elements such as part of the front and/or back tires.

HORIZONTAL OR VERTICAL

As you look through your viewfinder try turning the camera both vertical and horizontal to change the look of your photo. An example may be if want to do a shot with a lighthouse in the background turn your camera vertical so you can get closer to your bike without risking cutting off the top of the lighthouse rather than backing up to get everything which tends to make things much smaller than they need be. Experiment with horizontal and vertical camera positions before just snapping away. It only takes a second but can make all the difference in the final image. Don't forget about the "Rule of 3rd's" as it can be applied to both horizontal and vertical photos.

SUPPORT YOUR CAMERA

I always recommend supporting your camera properly to ensure a sharp clear photo. A good stance is the simplest way of doing this. Whether you are standing or crouching make sure to keep your elbows in close to your body. If your elbows are sticking out away from your body it is harder to keep the camera still. Also use both hands! Most cameras are designed to be held in the right hand so use your left hand to support the camera from the bottom. Be careful not to cover the flash with a stray finger! A tripod is best and there are many small lightweight ones available. It is not always practical to carry a tripod while traveling on a motorcycle so one sometimes must be creative. You can brace your camera on a fence post, hood of a car, a tree or anything that is solid. If you are lying on the ground for a low angle use your elbows to support yourself and your camera. A well supported camera ensures sharp, clear photos. With a bit of practice you will soon find a comfortable position that is best for you

WATCH YOUR BACKGROUND

Don't forget to look at what is around and behind the bike. Take a moment to make sure there aren't any garbage cans, loose garbage, power lines or other such distracting and unattractive items lurking about that could possibly ruin a good shot. If you want to have your bike fill most of the photo then try and keep your background simple and uncluttered. Buildings, solitary trees, swing sets and other everyday items are often overlooked and can distract from your subject, so be aware

If you wish to photograph your bike in a scenic shot such as in a beach scene, think about what elements of the scene you want to see and position your bike and yourself accordingly.

Photo Tip: These two photographs (right) have Province House in the background. While the first shows the building as most people view it, the second provides a more dramatic view of the columns framed by magnificent trees. To include bikes in the photo, bend down for the best perspective. The photos also demonstrate that by cutting out a dismal or grey sky, and using trees to fill in what would be dull sky, you get a much nicer picture.

CLEAN YOUR BIKE!

A quick wipe down will make your bike look better in photographs. It doesn't necessarily need a full wash and wax job but a once over with a towel can do wonders for bringing the sparkle back to the paint job and chrome features. Just be careful of hot pipes etc if you've been driving. Using Armor All or similar products on the tires, seat and grips will also help as it makes everything look more saturated and newer looking.

TO USE OR NOT TO USE THE FLASH

Most point and shoot cameras these days automatically turn the flash on when you turn on your camera. If your camera will allow try shooting one picture with your flash on and one with the flash off. Turning your flash off will force the camera to expose for the available light in the scene and you can decide later which look you prefer. Be sure the camera is well supported as shutter speeds will slow down causing camera shake and blurry pictures.

TRY A SILHOUETTE

For a dramatic shot try shooting a silhouette. The easiest way is to wait until sunset. Place your bike so that there is nothing but sky in behind it. You may have to crouch or even lay on the ground to get the best angle. Turn off your flash so that it won't light up the bike and the camera will expose for the sunset silhouetting the bike against the dramatic

near Confederation Bridge, Borden-Carleton
John Watson photos

evening sky. Try not to get the actual sun in your photo, or hide the sun behind your bike, for best results. Try shooting with your flash on as well. A little fill flash in a silhouette situation can result in very dramatic lighting. Again experiment.

Take the time to read your manual and always carry it with you. Most cameras allow for some control over the flash power. This lets you experiment with how much light the flash is putting out. Sometimes just a little extra light is much more pleasing and natural looking than a full power burst of the "automatic" setting.

BEACHES

Crystal Beach

Even though this is Canada's smallest province, Prince Edward Island probably has more miles of swimable, sand beaches than any other. There are at least 40 listed beaches and many are miles long. And, they are never more than a short ride away so grab your suit, towel and sun block and set out to "the shore."

PEI can fulfill almost any beach fantasy with miles of white sand backed by majestic dunes, or red sand backed by sculpted sandstone cliffs, to choose from. Private and isolated or tended by lifeguards with service areas, food and accommodation nearby, they are readily accessed. We even have beaches that "sing!" and some favoured by those seeking an "all-over" tan.

On the north shore, the most popular beaches are the white sand within the Prince Edward Island National Park in the area accessed through Cavendish and various points east to Dalvay, as well as those at Greenwich, accessed through St. Peters. Fully serviced areas, along with several smaller, more intimate beaches ensure you'll find what suits you. If you enjoy a good long walk venture west, towards the sandspit found at the western area of the park accessed at Cavendish. Be sure to take sun screen and a drink - it's a long walk to the end of the spit and back, but magical. Some areas may be fenced off, to preserve the nesting areas of the piping plover - please respect them.

The south shore also boasts many first class beaches. Red sand instead of white, often backed by red sandstone cliffs. Here sands often slop gently out from shore creating water temperatures even warmer than those on the north shore.

BEACHCOMBING

One of the best things to do on the beach is to stroll in the surf seeking treasures. Little bits of nature, or history washed ashore by the tides and waves. Now we all know you can't be carrying pieces of driftwood, or anything big, or stinky for that matter. Saddle bags just don't have that much room. We can enjoy the hunt, to see what we can find, and maybe gather up just 2 or 3 tiny treasures as keepsakes. Self-closing plastic bags are a must here. Last thing you want is sand or "eau du sea" in your saddle bags.

The best place to find shells and such is where sea and sand meet, particularly after a storm with onshore winds. This is also the time to keep your eyes peeled for Irish Moss harvesters who use heavy horses to rake up the seaweed.
A true photo op!

Prince Edward Island has always claimed bragrights for having the warmest salt water north of Florida - averaging 20 degrees Celcius (70 F). Most credit the Gulf Stream for bringing warm water, but I believe some of the credit goes to the fact that the shallow waters warm in the summer sun.

Many provincial and community beaches have supervised swimming areas. Seaside camping or nearby accommodation and eateries make any visit to the beach an enjoyable one which can be an integral part of Island vacations. **If you have a mind to explore, check out some of these Island gems:**

Hidden beaches such as this one north west of the East Point Lighthouse are common along our coasts

Cavendish, Brackley Beach, Dalvay and Green-wich within PEI National Park: Beaches are spectacular and well care for. White sand, marram grass covered dunes, sculpted red sandstone cliffs, sand spits and walking trails that bring you face to face with nature, interpretive displays and programs to increase your understanding and appreciation, and services such as washrooms, change houses, picnic areas and lifeguards are part of the package. Admission charged to the Park during the summer season. It is free in the spring and fall, and the beaches are less crowded, perfect time for walking.

Basin Head - accessed at the Basin Head Fisheries Museum near Souris, the glorious white sand beach, backed by dunes is famous for its ability to "sing." To explain: on wide, white sand beaches along P.E.I.'s eastern shore, the

MARINE PROTECTED AREA

As you drive into Basin Head Fisheries Museum (where you park to access the beach and facilities) you pass a lagoon which is a Marine Protected Area. Defined as a coastal or oceanic area given special status in order to protect and conserve the resources that live within it, the Basin Head ecosystem is inhabited by a rich diversity of plants, fish, mammals and birds. Most notable is a unique form of Irish Moss which has a life cycle and habitat limited to Basin Head. Now Irish Moss is a cash crop harvested around the province for the Carrageenan it contains which is used as a thickening agent in dairy products and cosmetics. The Basin Head variety yields 75% pure carrageenan versus the 45-50% found in the common form found in waters around the Island. This lagoon is also home to the American eel, a catadromous species of fish that spends most of its life in freshwater, but returns to the Sargasso Sea to spawn. Eels used to be an important food fish in pioneer times, but today declining populations, and changing tastes among human beings, have reduced fishing. Thankfully an eel management plan at national and international levels is working to secure the future of the snake-like fish.

ocean winds compacts the fine sand particles. Walking along undisturbed sand, scuffing bare feet, produces a squeak, or "singing" with each step. To get to this beach you have to cross the "race" , a narrow man made channel at the Basin Head Wharf using a bridge built for walkers (top photo).   Diving in at the freshwater upstream end of the millrace, swimmers are swept along a water joyride and gently deposited on the saltwater beach 100 metres away or sandbars. This has long been a favourite sport with local youngsters, but check with locals to be sure tide and water conditions are right before trying it yourself.

Cedar Dunes, the West Point Lighthouse towers over this beach located adjacent Cedar Dunes Provincial Park in western Prince Edward Island. A favourite walking beach for us, easily accessed from the lighthouse parking lot or the park, and a great place to enjoy the sea. You can often see the lights of New Brunswick in the evening. Check out the local legends in the lighthouse.

OUR DUNES ARE FRAGILE

The dunes and cliffs which surround Prince Edward Island are spectacular in their beauty and like many beautiful things fragile. We ask that everyone use designated access areas to our beautiful beaches, especially the white sand of the north shore. Many feet destroy the grasses and also the natural habitats of wildlife so please enjoy without destroying.

North Cape, at the extreme western end of the Island this is one of the best places to explore tide pools, and search the shore for bits and pieces of nature. Venture out on the reef - its magical to walk surrounded by the sea. Seals may accompany you. Sea birds will show the curve of the reef as the tide goes out. On shore explore the sculpted sandstone cliffs. Further around the point colonies of birds nesting in the cliffs will entertain if you take the time to observe.

Panmure Island, located north-east of Montague not really an island, but a causeway, with a white sand beach on the seaward side, and red sand across the road in the sheltered waters facing St. Mary's Bay. Caution: Take it easy on the causeway and carefully avoid clam shells on the road. Seagulls like to drop clams on the road, breaking the shell so they can feast on the critter inside. Those broken shells can puncture a tire.

The beaches and reef at North Cape make for excellent beachcombing. Many tide pools reveal marine life to enjoy watching.

Beware the Rip Current

CAUTION: - The waters surrounding our Island are nothing but tempting. But you must remember that swimming in the ocean, with the waves, and rip currents requires you to take some care. The sea is powerful, especially when the surf is up. Play in those waves and you will soon find that they can pull the sand right out from under your feet as the water receeds. Its fun, but also an indicator that you need to play safe.

The greatest danger to swimmers comes with a Rip Current. Caused by water rushing back out to sea between two sandbars a rip current can pull even the strongest swimmer out to sea. But they are relatively easy to escape as long at you do the right thing:
- If you find yourself being pulled out to sea DON'T PANIC. Relax and swim parallel to the shore. Soon the current will release you and you can swim back in. Never try to swim against a rip current. They are simply to strong.

We recommend swimming at supervised beaches. Check in with lifeguards when you reach the beach for daily conditions. Lifeguards supervise certain beaches within the PEI National Park, and Provincial Park beaches: Jacques Cartier, Cedar Dunes, Chelton Beach, Northumberland, Cabot Beach, Basin Head, Red Point and Panmure Island. Visitor Information Centres will have information about hours of supervision, locations and so on.

Rainy Day? Enjoy a 'wet' experience indoors......

You might want to take your swim indoors. Both Charlottetown and Summerside have top-notch aqua centres with frequent open swims. Getting wet indoors on a rainy day is a great thing to do, and just think. No sand in your bathing suit!

Charlottetown - The CARI Centre located at University of Prince Edward Island, off University Ave   569-4584
Summerside - Credit Union Place aquatic centre, 511 Notre Dame Street   432-1234

Or book into a hotel like Howard Johnstons Dutch Inn or Super 8 Charlottetown located in North River, just west of Charlottetown on Rte 1, or Loyalist Country Inn by Lakeview. They all have an indoor pool.

Strongman Hosts Island's Largest Rally

To define Tom Nicholls as the strong silent type is a surprisingly accurate statement. Tom, owner of Vacationland RV Park in Brackley Beach, host campground for the largest rally on the Island, is one of those behind the scenes guys who quietly goes about the business of making sure things are running smoothly. Not only does he, with the help of his wife, Brenda and staff, welcome up to 400 visiting motorcyclists to Island Rally late each summer, they also manage to integrate them into their campsites alongside the regulars at the campground and keep things running smoothly.

In fact they run Vacationland so well it was named one of the the top-rated parks for 2009 by Trailer Life Directory. To be chosen one of the top 300 from more than 12,000 parks in the network is quite an achievement!

On the strong side, Tom is a strongman. A real one. A powerlifter, he garnered many awards in his chosen sport. The last time we wrote about Tom the strapping strongman had just returned home from the Canadian national power lifting championships, held in British Columbia, a multiple winner. As a result of competing in the 125 kg Masters Mens category, where he bench pressed 245 kg (539 lbs), hoisted 330 kg (726 lbs) in the squat, and dead-lifted 340.5 kg (750.5 lbs) - thereby setting a new Canada record, with a total of 915 kg (2,013 lbs!) - he won his 10th consecutive victory.

"I was coming off an injury, and hadn't trained for four weeks," he explains, "so I had to pull it together quickly. I still managed to set a deadlift record. I felt I could have lifted more, but you learn to listen to your body. You don't recover as quickly, and you say, 'Be smart. Walk away."

Although no longer competing Nicholls can proudly point to the fact that he'd lifted more than any person in Canada. Especially notable is his Master Lifter title, which is calculated mathematically by comparing the weight of the competitor vs. the weight lifted. Nicholls held the title of Master Lifter Male, for several years. He held several records in his weight class and was getting ready to return to the Masters to represent Canada

Now over 40, Tom is devoting more time to his bride, and to a favourite activity, motorcycling. While he loves cruising the roads on his full-dresser we have also spotted him out with the dirt bike crowd riding the clay back roads of the Island in the fall.

He says he loves the bike, and takes every opportunity to ride, even if its just from home to the campgrounds.

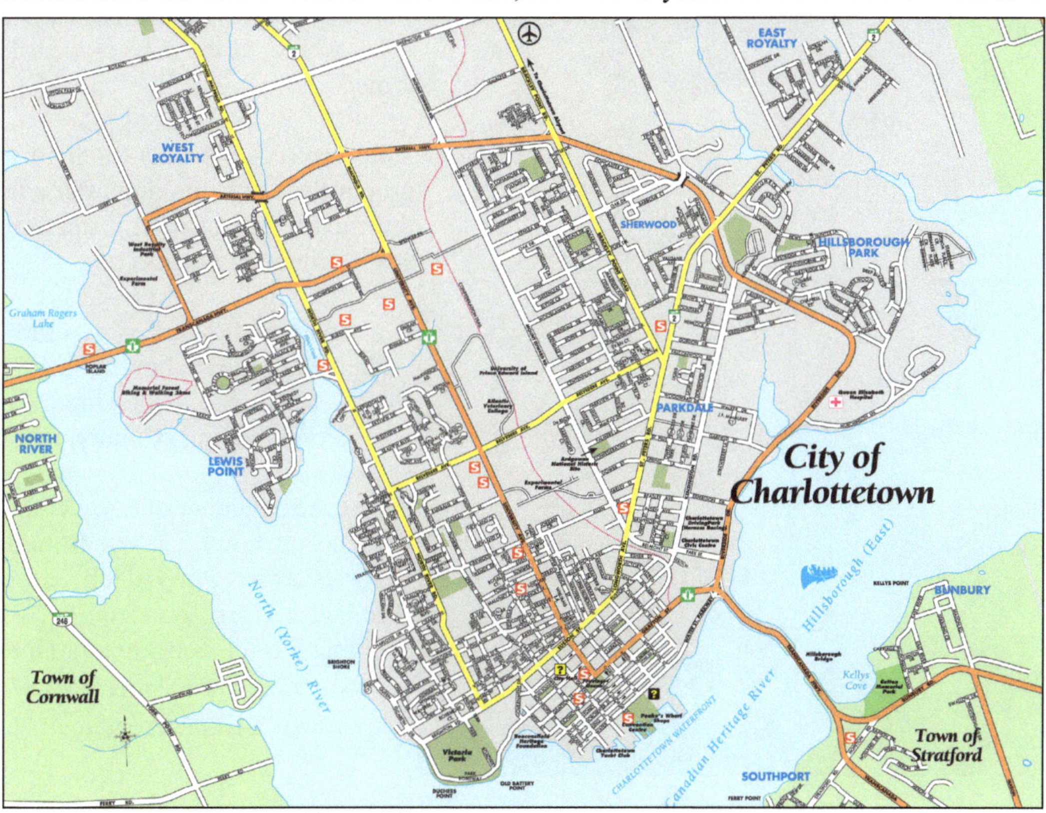

HORSE POWER ABUNDANT ON PEI

by Debbie Gamble:

If you tire of your steel horses, and have a hankering for real horses instead, there's lots of horse power available on PEI. From harness racing to hunter/jumpers, from miniature horses to the gentle giants in horse pulls, there's a horse activity to suit just about anyone.

Of course, the pinnacle of horse-power shows on PEI is the provincial exhibition, known as Old Home Week, usually held in mid-August. This week-long affair offers livestock exhibitions, midway, concerts, and of course, horse shows. You'll finda myriad different horse events at OHW: horse pulls, cattle penning, reining, pleasure classes – both western and english - harness classes, miniature horse classes. All there, for your viewing pleasure.

Harvesting Irish Moss (above) and heavy horses in Western Prince Edward Island (below)

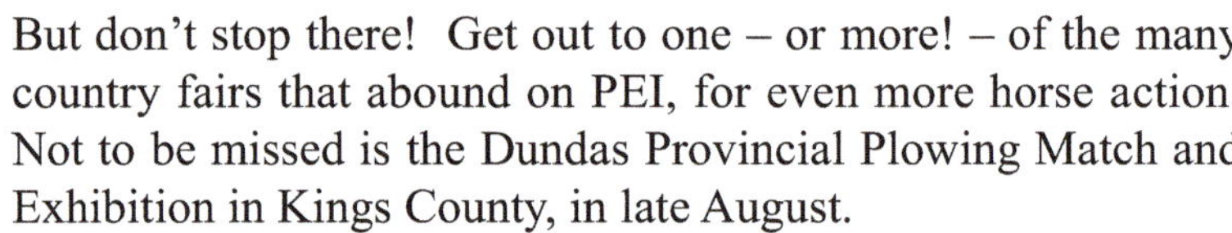

And don't miss a card of harness racing! Thrill to the roar of the crowd, as the field of racers rounds the upper turn and drives for the wire. It's horsepowered excitement with a capital E! Major tracks are located in Charlottetown and Summerside.

There are a number of smaller, "matinee" tracks on PEI, each offering their own unique flavour of racing ... for example, the Pinette Raceway in eastern PEI, which hosts the annual Kilted Pace, where all the drivers wear kilts! And a training facility in Tyne Valley

And there is a Harness Racing Camp, where you can become a groom for a day, looking after a horse and actually driving it on the track. For more information, contact: (902) 894-6511 or www.peimatineetracks.com.

But don't stop there! Get out to one – or more! – of the many country fairs that abound on PEI, for even more horse action. Not to be missed is the Dundas Provincial Plowing Match and Exhibition in Kings County, in late August.

There are a number of horse clubs on PEI, and they all hold their own horse shows. Choose from the Western Horse Association, Charlottetown Pony Club, Horse Trials PEI, Dressage PEI, Miniature Horse Association, PEI Team Penning Inc, Island Reining Association, Quarter Horse Association, Hunter/Jumper Association or the Paint Horse Association. Find out more at: http://www.islandhorsecouncil.ca/

Horses are such an integral part of PEI, which has been called the "Kentucky of Canada" because we boast more horses per capita than any other province. Being an agricultural province with a rich heritage, of course draft horses played a big part in our past.

As you drive around our verdant countryside, you'll see many draft horses in the fields, or perhaps you'll be lucky, on a coastline drive up west, and see some horses and their owners ploughing through the waves as they harvest Irish Moss. The moss is dried and processed for the carragheen it contains. (This ingredient is used in all manner of goods, i.e., ice cream, lipstick, etc.)

And if you want to really get in on the action, and mount a flesh-and-blood "horsepower unit", there are a few trail riding establishments on the Island, offering rides at reasonable rates They'll take you over gentle Island terrain, through woods, across lush fields, and even along the shore. You'll love it!

If a more sedate pace suites you book a horse and carriage ride in Charlottetown, Avonlea Village in Cavendish, or at the Anne of Green Gables Museum located in Park Corner.

So, when you crave real horses, hop on your steel horses and head on out to one of the many horse events or activities to be found on PEI. Happy trails!

Photo Tip: Keep your eyes peeled for horses grazing in fields as you travel the Island. They provide a wonderful focal point for scenic photos.

Interesting to know.....

As part of its mandate to interpret the history of agriculture Orwell Corner Historic Village, located on Rte 1 east of Stratford, operates a small living farm where the work is performed using horse power and turn of the century farming methods. The horse power for the farm is supplied by a team of rare Canadian horses who came to Orwell from Fortress Louisburg. Two foals have been added to the "herd" which includes a Belgian, Dot, who has mentored the younger animals in the fine art of ploughing and fertilizing fields, cultivating crops, demonstrating harnessing and offering wagon rides to visitors. A visit to the farm will give you an understanding and appreciation of agriculture and rural life on Prince Edward Island in the 1890's. The area was settled by Scots and later Irish and United Empire Loyalists. A wonderful place to gain an appreciation for life in a by gone era.

Country Fairs and Exhibitions

by Debbie Gamble

There's an excitement in the air of Prince Edward Island come early summer: that's when the fine weather and longer days portend the arrival of country fairs and exhibitions taking place over the summer season.

A mind-boggling combination of livestock exhibitions, horse classes, food competitions, horticultural shows, midway rides and entertainment, Island country fairs can fill the bill if you crave a different way to spend some of your leisure time.

The Summerside Lobster Carnival kicks off the fun in early July. Of course, lobster is king at this carnival, but there is a wide variety of fun things to do and see, including the Sink or Swim cardboard boat races.

Crapaud Exhibition at the end of July features concerts, farm livestock and 4-H competitions, horse shows, craft displays, and some of the best home-made cuisine available on PEI. Just a few days later, horse-power of another kind roars into the community with the arrival of the PEI Tractor Pulls.

Old Home Week, the grand-daddy exhibition of them all, takes the spotlight in mid August. Watch the harness races - don't miss the Gold Cup & Saucer race! - stroll the midway, marvel at the wide variety of crafts on display in the Women's Institute competitions, sample Island foods, pit your knowledge against that of the judges in the livestock and horse classes, or partake of the daily family-themed live entertainment. There's something for everyone at Old Home Week!

The third week in August is the time for the Kensington Harvest Festival. Crowned by the Miss Community Gardens pageant, it also features a 25 km marathon event, a parade, a pancake breakfast, talent search, and lots more over this 5-day long event.

Eastern PEI is the focus in late August, for the Dundas Fair and Exhibition, one of the oldest country fairs on PEI. It's main "claim to fame" is that Dundas is the host of an international plowing match. Watch the expert ploughmen (and women) turn the sod, both by tractor and by old-fashioned horse-power. Concerts, horse shows and a Queen of the Furrows competition are also on the agenda.

Horse pulls at Dundas Fair and Exhibition

Up west at the end of August, in Mont Carmel you'll find the L'Exposition Agricole et Le Festival Acadien. In addition to the events found at other exhibitions, they have a pole-climbing event, a strongman competition, and 3 & 4-wheeler pulls, all with that Island Acadian flavour!

Up in Souris, the Eastern Kings Exhibition in mid-September rounds out the fairs and exhibitions line-up. Claiming to be the oldest fair on PEI, it offers livestock and craft displays, food sampling (including homemade ice-cream!), cake auction, entertainment, an antique tractor competition, and much more.

No matter what the area, or what your interest, there's a country fair or exhibition that will allow you to partake of your favourite past-time. Park your pegs at a country exhibition – see you at the fair! 

Mud Red Island Musical Montage

by Debbie Gamble

If music is your passion (the other one, besides motorcycling, we mean!), then PEI has a real treat in store for you! You will find music to sooth the soul, tap the toe, and every mood in between.

Prince Edward Island has a long and loving musical history. New Islanders came from many places, bringing their musical heritage with them. And so it is that, today, you can partake of musical styles ranging from Celtic (Irish and Scottish) and Acadian French (both wildly popular) to old-time country, new country, pop, rock, grunge, heavy metal, Christian, easy listening, jazz and so on. A good resource for finding your favourite musical style and the venue offering it, is to get a current copy of the free publication, The Buzz. It tells you who's playing where, around the Island.

Victoria Row in Charlottetown's downtown.   John Watson photo

Not to be missed on your visit is a good old Island Kitchen Party. Past tradition holds that folks – usually farming and fishing families – would gather at someone's home on a Saturday evening. Everyone would bring some food, and the musicians their instruments, and would have a high old time in the kitchen, taking turns playing and singing, and scoffing up the culinary offerings. (Some of the best parties we've ever attended were kitchen parties.)

These days, kitchen parties are more organized affairs. Many communities have regular musical evenings, sometimes called ceilidhs (pronounced KAY-lees) which welcome all comers. For a small admission fee, you'll have an evening jam-packed with some of the best Island entertainers and musicians, and you'll probably get a lunch at evening's end, as well!

The Club scene thrives in Charlottetown during the summer. Two favourites are the Olde Dublin Pub and Peake's Quay, owned by Harley riders Liam and Kim Dolan. Entertainment varies from the best of local to touring singers and musicians.

Both Charlottetown and Cavedish are gaining a great reputation for concerts with stars such as the Black Eyed Peas and Taylor Swift. Check it out.

Great places to experience our music are the many festivals, ceileighs, and concerts held around the Island. We have fiddle, country music, rock and traditional festivals. Come and explore our musical roots!

ACCOMMODATIONS

Prince Edward Island offers a complete range of accommodations from bed & breakfasts to luxury resorts, from rustic camping to cottages by the sea, from city hotels to hostels. The following accommodations are active supporters of the motorcycle touring community. We ask that you consider supporting them when making your accommodation choice. And do tell them you found their information through MotorcyclePEI.

BRACKLEY BEACH:
Millstream Cottages and Motel
On Rte. 15 at Brackley Beach
Conveniently located
P: 902 672-2186   Toll Free: 1-800-668-8897
 info@millstream.pe.ca   www.millstream.pe.ca

Vacationland RV Park
East off Rte. 2 at
Brackley Beach
Camping-hosts of annual Island Rally
P: 902 672-2317   Toll-free: 1-800-529-0066
moreinfo@vacationlandrv.pe.ca
www.vacationlandrv.pe.ca or www.vacationlandrv.ca

CHARLOTTETOWN:
Canada's Best Value Inn and Suites
20 Capital Dr., (on the TransCanada Hwy)
Charlottetown, PE   C1E 1E7
902 892-2481   Toll Free: 1-877-890-2481
www.canadabestvalueinnpei.com

CORNWALL:
Hyde Away House B&B
196 Upper MeadowBank Rd.
Cornwall, PE C0A 1H0
Levina and Herman Luymes
902 566-2378
levinaluymes@hotmail.com   bbcanada.com/10317.html

NEW LONDON:
New London Bay Motel
10539, Rt. 6,
New London
Toll Free:1-866-786-2234 (reservations)
newlondonbaymotel@pei.aibn.com
www.newlondonbaymotel.net

NORTH BEDEQUE:
Canada's Best Value Inn/Country Pines Inn & Suites
Rte. 1A, between North Bedeque and Summerside
Kathy and Bill McInnis and family
Mail: 79 All Weather Hwy., Summerside, PE C1N 5L3
P: 436-5564 Toll free: 1-866-494-5233
www.thecountrypines.com   kbmcinnis@pei.eastlink.ca

NORTH RIVER:
Howard Johnson Dutch Inn
100 Trans Canada Highway, RR#4,
Cornwall, C0A 1H0
Toll-free: 1-800-915-4656
P: 902-566-2211 F: 902-566-2214
email@hojopei.com   www.hojopei.com

Super 8 Charlottetown "Hog the Island" special
Kirk MacDonald, General Manager
15 York Rd. (Rte 248) just off the TransCanada
Cornwall   C0A 1H0
P: 902-892-7900   F: 902-892-5533
www.super8.com

SUMMERSIDE:
Loyalist Country Inn by Lakeview
195 Harbour Drive
Summerside PEI C1N 5R1
Ph: 902.436.3333   Toll Free: 877.355.3500
lakeviewhotels.com/

TEA HILL:
The Birches Housekeeping Cottages
On Rte 1A, east of Stratford
1517 Pownal Road at Alexandra Point
Cottages 10 km east of Charlottetown
902 569-4293   Toll free: 1-800-463-4293
www.thebirchescottages.ca
Town amenities in a country setting. Wireless internet

TIGNISH:
Tignish Heritage Inn
(behind St. Simon and St. Jude Church, off Maple St.)
Box 98, Tignish, PE C0B 2B0
902 882-2491 F: 902 882-2500
Toll Free: 1-877-882-2491
heritageinn@tignish.com   www.tignish.com/inn

WEST POINT:
West Point Lighthouse Inn, Museum
Rte 14 and 364 Cedar Dunes Park Rd.
West Point, PEI
902 859-3605   Toll Free: 1-800-764-6854
westpointlighthouse@gmail.com
www.westpointlighthouse.com

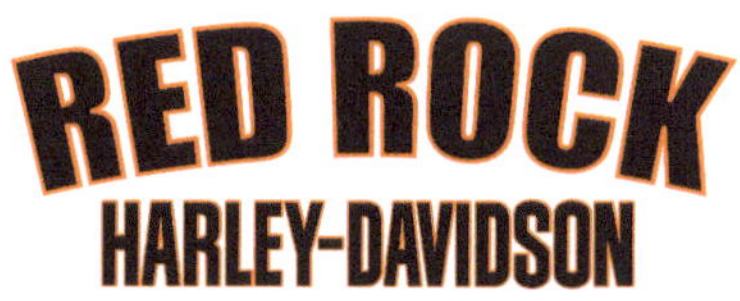

Prince Edward Island's only authorized Harley-Davidson retailer

18 Warren Grove Rd., at Hwy 1
North River, P.E.I.
Phone: 902 368-8324
Fax: 902 368-7191
www.redrockharleydavidson.com

Sales . Service . Parts.

Come visit our showroom with its great stock of Harley-Davison motorcycles, genuine parts and a large selection of accessories. Authorized Harley-Davidson gift and clothing boutique. Collectibles. Full service with factory trained technicians.

To book appointments for service, etc. visit www.redrockharleydavidson.com or call 368-8324 Open 8:30 am-5:30 pm M-F, 9-1 Sat, during July & Aug 9-4 Sat) Red Rock hosts rides and events, so check out the bulletin boards to see whats happening.

Toy Master Motor Sports

Kawasaki - Let the good times roll

5 Campbell Rd, off Rte. 2,
Winsloe, P.E.I. C1E 1Z2
Phone: 902 894-5287 Fax: 902 368-1812 After hours:
902 626-6344
Email: gary@toymaster.ca
www.toymaster.ca

Recreational vehicle specialist.

P.E.I.'s only full line retailer for Kawasaki. Motorcycles, dirt bikes, ATVs, watercraft and snowmobiles. Genuine manufacturer parts and accessories to keep your toy running smoothly. Service you can trust. Trained service technicians are continuously updating their skills with training provided by the manufacturers. Full line of clothing: Kawasaki, Joe Rocket, leathers, t-shirts, fleece, hats. 5 Year warranties and on the spot financing available. Locally owned and operated for 16 years. Drop in to their store in Winsloe.

CHARLOTTETOWN & AREA:

Red Rock Harley-Davidson
18 Warren Grove Rd., at Hwy 1
North River
authorized Harley-Davidson retailer
P: 902 368-8324
F: 902 368-7191
www.redrockharleydavidson.com

DBL Dream Machines
451 Mount Edward Road
Charlottetown, PE   C1E 2A1
Honda dealer, full service
P: 902 368-2527   F: 902 620-7234
dblhonda@bellaliant.com
www.dbldreammachines.com

Toy Master Motor Sports
5 Campbell Rd, off Rte. 2,
Winsloe
Kawasaki
P: 902 894-5287   F: 902 368-1812
After hours: 902 626-6344
Email:gary@toymaster.ca
www.toymaster.ca

SUMMERSIDE :

Centennial Auto, Sport & Tire
616 South Drive
Summerside
Suzuki
P: 902 436-1022   F: 902 436-1066
tim@centennialast.com
www.centennialast.com

Food and Drink

Hungry? Dine at first class restaurants, or enjoy lobster on the wharf, just steps from the fishing boats that harvested it from the sea. Visit our markets where organic and traditional family farmers, along with ethnic food booths, extend a warm welcome. Check out our culinary school; one of the finest in Canada, whose students bring home Olympic and World gold medals. They dish up great cuisine at the school restaurant. Bottom line. In Prince Edward Island food and drink is much more than chowing down at the nearest fast food. It is an experience to savour and enjoy.

Touring can build up a great appetite. No question. Happily huge opportunity to indulge yourself exists in Prince Edward Island with great grub, be it a casual pub style meal, a lobster supper, a road side snack stop, or fine dining. Heck we also have all of the usual fast food, but for now lets focus on the special-to-PEI experience.

No trip to Prince Edward Island is complete without a true effort to enjoy local seafood. Surrounded by water we have some of the finest shellfish in the world. Fishermen and women harvest lobster, clams, scallops and fish. Marine farmers grow mussels, oysters, clams and even scallops. The aquaculture industry is very visible as you tour the Island, watch the bays and rivers for rows of floats - those floats are holding "socks" of mussels. The Island is one of the world's major producers of cultured mussels.

It just stands to reason that a ready supply of seafood means lots of talented cooks will offer it up on their menus. We also have a thriving agricultural community. As you travel our highways you will pass fields filled with potatoes, fruits and vegetables, which are brought to you at many markets, roadside stands and restaurants that are dedicated to using local ingredients. Without doubt it is the finer restaurants or those with strong links to community that are the most dedicated to using local ingredients.

We also have a number of specialty producers who create products you will want to enjoy, and take home. Most ship so it's a perfectly logical thing to do! For starters one of our innovative chocolate shops produces chocolate covered potato chips which are pretty awesome; as well as lots of specialty chocolates. You can watch chocolates being made at Anne of Green Gables Chocolates at Avonlea Village in Cavendish. Not far away, in New Glasgow, watch the Prince Edward Island Preserve Company produce jams right on site. Not far away, at Cheeselady's Gouda in Winsloe North, cheese makers will give you a look at the cheese making process right on the farm.

Thankfully you are in a place where most tastes can be satisfied, although you may have to search out ethnic restaurants in larger centers - this is a small province. Charlottetown is your best bet, particularly the farmers market.

The culinary winners here will be the folks who are eager to sample the fare that is unique to a region.

Small eateries in small communities won't have the huge selection found in larger places, but you will find more homemade and hopefully more use of local ingredients. There are few things to equal mussels in St. Peters, or lobster fresh from the sea in West Point, or delightful meat pies from a small inn in Kensington, or pan-fried trout you caught with your own hands in Bellevue, or handmade chocolates in Victoria, or oysters at the Island's first oyster bar, Claddagh Oyster House in Charlottetown, or, well, the list just goes on and on.

Most Visitor Information Centres have listings of restaurants in their area as well as copies of menus with prices, so drop in ask. There is a brochure, the Prince Edward Island Restaurant and Menu Guide, available at Visitor Information Centres. If you like to seek out culinary adventures check it out, along with the Buzz, local newspapers and the PEI Visitors Guide.

Paul Offer, The Doctors Inn in Tyne Valley, a regular at Charlottetown Farmers Market.

CELEBRATING OUR BEST
– fun foody festivals and stuff

A fun food experience can be found at festivals and events that celebrate some of our best Island foods. The top show of them all brings you in at what many say is the best time of year, mid-September. The PEI International Shellfish Festival (photos to right) not only serves up mussels, oysters, clams, and lobster. It also features world-class level oyster shucking competitions, an International Chowder competition that attracts chefs from around the world, mussel socking, and culinary demonstrations; and great entertainment. Other events? Here is a sampling:

> Lobster Carnival in Summerside
> PEI Potato Blossom Festival in O'Leary
> Northumberland Provincial Fisheries Festival in Murray Harbour
> Tyne Valley Oyster Festival in Cornwall
> St. Peters Wild Blueberry Festival & Homecoming
> Island Chocolates Company Chocolate Festival in Victoria
> Fall Flavours - Prince Edward Island
> Culinary Boot Camps

FIRST CANADIAN WORLD CHAMPS

Students of the Culinary Institute of Canada in Charlottetown brought home the first ever Canadian World Championship win when Youth Team Canada were name World Champions at the 2007 Knorr World Junior Grand Prix held in Scotland. The competition was a stepping stone to the 2008 World Culinary Olympics held in Germany where they once again represented Canada and brought home gold! Competition is an important element of education at the Institute, a plus for culinarians. Producing Olympians and World Champions takes dedication and practice which students get by cooking and serving in the schools fine dining restaurant, The Lucy Maud Dining Room, in Charlottetown.

CELEBRITY CHEF

Prince Edward Island is the home for celebrity chef Michael Smith, whose television shows appear on the Food Networks. Inn Chef, Chef at Large, Chef at Home, and Chef Abroad are all produced right here on the Island. Chef Michael is a true supporter of Island cuisine and often spotted at culinary events, or filming his TV shows. He spearheaded a fall culinary festival held in October with many fun activities around the Island.

POTATOES

Every where you travel on PEI you will see field after field of potatoes. Those fields can be a thing of beauty, with their neatly tended rows of green plants and red soil. A photographers delight, they have a much more important role in Island life. The industry has faced many changes over the years, even so it has been the foundation of many family farms, as potatoes were grown for both food and seed. As well PEI has been a leader in research and development. Their importance goes beyond a great product that is exported to many parts of the world. Potatoes feed the hungry, in fact one acre of potatoes can feed far more people than an acre of grain. There is a school of thought that potatoes, rich in vitamin C and potassium, could help stop poverty and malnutrition in the world. They are the fourth largest source of food, after rice, wheat, and maize. During WWII a dehydration plant in Summerside made potato products to ship to war-torn Europe. The best place to learn fascinating stuff about the spud, which isn't lowly at all, is the Prince Edward Island Potato Museum in O'Leary.

DRINKS

Those who like to imbibe the good stuff, will find a few treasures on this Island of ours.

Rossignol Estate Winery in Little Sands has won many awards for its premium table wines. It's a lovely ride along the south shore, east of Wood Islands. The farm winery-by-the-sea and art gallery are backed by a beautiful view of Northumberland Strait.

Heading north to Rollo Bay drop in to Myriad View Artisan Distillery. Tour and witness "Strait Shine" as you learn about the Island tradition of moonshine.

The Prince Edward Distillery, in Hermanville is one of the few places in the world that is actually making potato vodka. Certainly the one such distillery in Canada, it uses 100% PEI spuds in the process. Take a tour and learn the process. It includes samples! We preferred the blueberry vodka.

Gahan House, a brewery, pub and mercantile produces PEI's only premium handcrafted ales and an opportunity to tour their in-house brewery in Historic Charlottetown.

If you are a wine connoisseur, there are several restaurants with good wine lists including the Claddagh Oyster House (upstairs, Olde Dublin Pub has a fine beer selection including lots of imports) and the Lucy Maud Dining Room at the Culinary Institute of Canada, both in Charlottetown.

There are liquor stores in many communities and at the entrance points to the Island, Borden-Carleton and Wood Islands. For a listing of liquor stores go to the Prince Edward Island Visitors Guide.

COFFEE STOPS

Coffee stops are as much a part of life in Prince Edward Island as the sun rising every morning. Islanders do enjoy their coffee, or tea. But even more they enjoy the camaraderie of being able to sit and talk to like minded folks for a while. Watching out for bikes in a coffee shop parking lot almost guarantees you will find like-minded folks inside (or out) ready for a chat.

One coffee shop stands out above all others for the welcome it extends to bikers. Bakin'Donuts in Summerside has even built special seating on a deck outside. There are a number of Bakin Donut stops in communities which are listed on page 57. We urge you to pull in and check out the friendly service.

Rossignol Estate Winery in Little Sands

Interesting to Know...how to eat lobster

Our introduction to lobster as a finger food was at the most basic level. Layers of newspaper covered the table, a chopping block, a cleaver and a roll of paper towels.Its that easy. We know you won't have a chopping block or cleaver in your saddle bag. Nevertheless you can still enjoy lobster. Picnic table recommended. Newspaper is good, and paper towels. Just stop at one of the many outlets located on wharfs, or nearby. Ask for lobster cooked, and cracked. You can get to the luscious meat without having it cracked but it can be hard on fingers and teeth. A hammer, a large knife, nutcrackers, even a smallspoon help, as do strong hands.

　　　To eat lobster break the shell apart, and dig out the meat. Just watch the points on the shell, they can inflict painful damage. It can be messy, but such fun! Twist the tail sideways from the body, then squeeze the sides together, then apart. Remove the black vein down the back of the meat. Twist claws off the body, and break the knuckles off from the claws. This is where the spoon or something similar (even a screw driver works) comes into play. Stick it into the joint and twist, then use it to scoop out the meat. The claws can be very hard to break. Twist off the thumb, then lay the claw flat on the table and whack it. Use a closed fist or a rock if need be. You might want to put on a leather glove, or lay a cloth over the claw. Make sure you hit the flat part. There is meat to be found in the body, just lift the back off and start searching.

　　　If all this crackin' and diggin' doesn't appeal a visit to a lobster supper, or even a lobster roll will give you a taste of PEI's favourite finger food. We do hope you take home many happy memories of Prince Edward Island, including great rides, great people met, great food and great times. Be sure to come back now!

Meet the Team

Motorcycle Touring in Prince Edward Island is published by Seacroft, in Prince Edward Island, Canada

Seacroft is a small home based business, producing and marketing books and printed products, developing websites, sharing knowledge through workshops, and striving to encourage and assist others. Owned and operated by Julie V. Watson, Seacroft reflects her approach to life.

Julie has wide and varied interests and loves to follow the path to adventure. Thus her interest in motorcycling has been added to an impressive list of published works delving into topics such as ghosts and shipwrecks, entrepreneurship, history, food and travel. She has produced a number of self-help books dealing with living with diabetes, making money through small business and more. She enjoys working with friends and family on printed products as well as presenting workshops for writers, those wishing to publish books and budding entrepreneurs. To check out various books and products produced by Seacroft go to www.seacroftpei.com or watch out for Julie at craft fairs and other events in Prince Edward Island.

Our motorcycling team includes:
　　　Publisher, head writer, designer and whip cracker - Julie V. Watson   www.seacroftpei.com
　　　Photographer and writer - John C. Watson   www.imps.ca
　　　Contributing writer - Debbie Gamble
　　　Assistant, web master and general supporter - Helen Grant
　　　Distribution - Jack Watson   biz@seacroftpei.com

Julie V. Watson
-publisher/writer

People have asked me where my love of motorcycle touring came from, especially as we have had to give it up to a large degree due to health problems. Early memories of being in a sidecar watching water splash higher and higher up the sides started it. Looking up at my father I could see he was enjoying himself and so was my mother behind him. Their smiles convinced my toddler brain that this was fun - so I laughed too. I spent my early years in post WWII England. Dad had courted Mom on a motorcycle.

Early family albums have pictures of them exploring the English countryside, ports and such. Our little family often picniced in the country. A favourite spot was beside a river which required one to ford, or drive through it, to get there. At that time in England fords through shallow rivers or brooks were commonplace. Thus the early memory. My parents had a busy bakery in Oxfordshire. Memories switch to traveling in a bread van. They took out the racks for holding bread to convert it into a camper of sorts. I remember sitting on a sun warmed stone wall overlooking a loch in Scotland. The land, which fell away toward the glistening blue water below, was covered by purple heather. The sight, scent and sounds of buzzing bees, and my parents preparing tea on their naptha gas stove have stayed with me all of my life. After emigrating to Canada they purchased a 1943 Buick. We explored the eastern seaboard of the United States, and much of Ontario in that big old car. Those nomadic expeditions fostered my love of being on the road.

I had the good fortune to marry a guy with a spirit of adventure - and motorcycling. After a few years away from riding while we focused on raising our son we got back at it. A move to Prince Edward Island from Ontario and a stint with real horses later we became empty nesters and returned to our love for motorcycles. Jack and I enjoyed great touring on the bike but health problems brought about change. We sold our house, purchased a Class B RV and plan to head on down the road. A new bike is hopefully in our future but it won't be a full dresser, BMW tour bike. We won't travel two-up for long distances, but can enjoy short day trips out from the campgrounds. In some regions, such as British Columbia, there are opportunities to rent bikes for day trips, as we happily found. I have to tell you, the adventurous side of us cranked up at the bike shows where we got a close look at side cars. They sure look like fun!

These days the business has grown to include all of our family and a number of good friends. Husband Jack works with the distribution side of things and any number of tasks we assign him. Our son is our prime photographer and contributor to the written side of things. We consider ourselves fortunate to be able to work together.

We don't know what the future holds. But we do know we'll tackle it head on. We came to the realization years ago that change is part of life. One has to adapt to what fate throws at you and find enjoyment how and where you can. That my friends is what it is all about, and why we started our web sites and tour guides: to help fellow enthusiasts focus on small pleasures, on great experiences, on enjoying life however and where ever they can. We wish you all safe travel, grand adventures, joy in the simple wonders of life, and most of all the good health and spirit to make the best of what you find before you each and every day.

John C. Watson
– Photographer/Writer

At just eight years of age John Watson purchased his first camera while vacationing with his parents. He's had a camera in his hand ever since.

John began his professional career as a weekend photographer for the local newspaper in Charlottetown, Prince Edward Island when he was just fifteen years of age. He continued to work in the field while pursuing formal training at Holland College in Charlottetown. John opened Imagemaker Photographic Studio in 1989. In 1993 he relocated IMPS to Vancouver, British Columbia but retains ties with Prince Edward Island, often returning to the region on assignment or working electronically with clients across the country.

 "With today's technologies and the internet I can set up shots in my Vancouver studio and e-mail them almost anywhere for consultation and approval before finalizing the shoot," says John.

His experience producing top quality photographs in the editorial, commercial and photojournalism fields have led to assignments from Alaska to Israel and many points in between. John has been hired as an accredited press photographer for three royal tours, has photographed local and international musical acts and Rock n' Roll Hall of Fame inductees. His work on a USO tour took him through Belgium, Israel, Turkey, Bahrain and Oman with rock and roll legend Joan Jett.

He has covered both local and international conferences, provided head-shots to actors and corporate leaders. John's photographs have appeared on the covers of books and magazines in Hong Kong, the UK, USA, Canada and Europe, as well as gracing the inside pages of many publications around the world.

John's interest in photographing motorcycles came through his parents who are biking enthusiasts. He often works with his mother, a writer and publisher, combining their talents to produce books, magazine articles and commercial projects. When she turned to writing about motorcycles, producing print materials (brochures etc) and web sites John continued to photograph bikes, bikers, the things they do and the places they visit.

John is known for sharing his expertise, and being willing to help others with photography. He gives private lessons in basic photography, using your camera (how to make the camera work for you), darkroom work and digital photography. He also gives workshops and been a guest speaker at numerous conferences. John also leads tours, taking photography enthusiasts into the field for a day with a pro.

"Like all creative fields photography requires constant attention to learning, expanding skill levels and to keeping abreast of both customer and technological trends and developments," says John. "It is both fulfilling and necessary to always ensure that I can provide the best service and product to my clients."

To learn more about John and his work
go to www.imps.ca

Debbie Gamble
– Writer

had a long break between her teenage experience with motorcycles and a re-introduction to riding in her 40s when motorcycling began to figure prominently in her life.

A true enthusiast, Debbie especially enjoys the people she meets along the way. "Motorcycling is a lifestyle that appeals to people from students to empty nesters, from all walks of life. We all share a bond - that love of being on the road, even if just for an hour or two a week."

When asked what attracts so many to this free-wheeling form of travel she says "The joy comes from the sense of unity and the sensory overload  riding provides; you relax and notice things you wouldn't in a four-wheel vehicle. Although tour motorcycling may seem a solitary recreation to the non-biker it is in fact a very social community of individuals who seem to enjoy talking about rides taken and rides planned, as much as actually traveling. The sense of camaraderie is hard to equal."

As a member of the PEI Motorcycle Touring Club (PEIMTC), she got involved in many activities including Island Rally, organizing runs, and does the club web page. She also worked with the Gold Wing Road Riders regional rally and held office with the Atlantic Regional Roadriders Council, s and on the board of the Motorcyclists Confederation of Canada, a national advocacy organization that champions motorcycling interests.

She wrote professionally about motorcycling for magazines and contributed to websites and our blog, http://blog.motorcyclepei.com/. She has written a book about horses, magazine articles, as well as many other topics. Debbie strives to keep her 1985 Honda 450 Nighthawk up and running for the riding season.